DESIGNS OF GATES

PUSTAK MAHAL®

Administrative office and sale centre
J-3/16 , Daryaganj, New Delhi-110002
☎ 23276539, 23272783, 23272784 • *Fax:* 011-23260518
E-mail: info@pustakmahal.com • *Website:* www.pustakmahal.com

Branches
Bengaluru: ☎ 080-22234025 • *Telefax:* 080-22240209
E-mail: pustak@airtelmail.in • pustak@sancharnet.in
Mumbai: ☎ 022-22010941, 022-22053387
E-mail: rapidex@bom5.vsnl.net.in
Patna: ☎ 0612-3294193 • *Telefax:* 0612-2302719
E-mail: rapidexptn@rediffmail.com

ISBN 978-81-223-0525-8

Edition: 2014

Printed at : Radha Offset Delhi

DESIGNS OF GATES

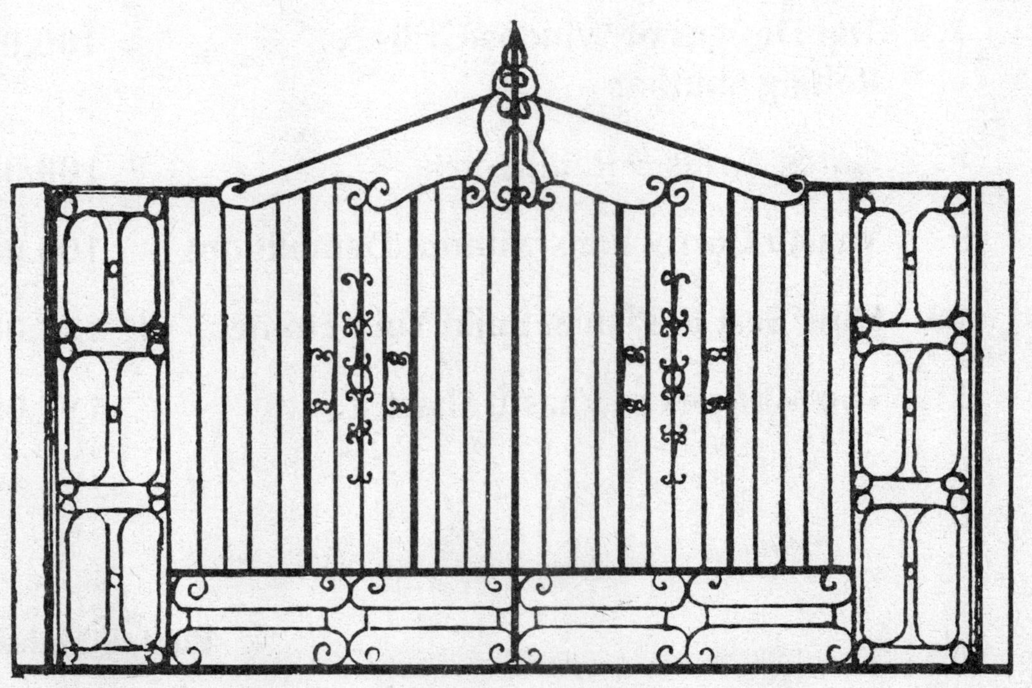

Other books in this series

1.	New Steel Furniture Catalogue	195.00
2.	More and More Designs of Gates, Grills, Railings & Staircases	100.00
3.	Designs of Railings	100.00
4.	Designs of Railings	100.00
5.	Designs of Windows	100.00
6.	Designs of Gates	100.00
7.	Top Designs of Windos Grills & Rolling Shutters	100.00
8.	Gates, Grills & Railing Sets	100.00
9.	Vaastu Corrections without Demolitions	100.00
10.	How Best to Plan & Build Your Home	175.00
11.	The Miracles of Vaastu Shastra	195.00

Pustak Mahal

Beautiful Gate

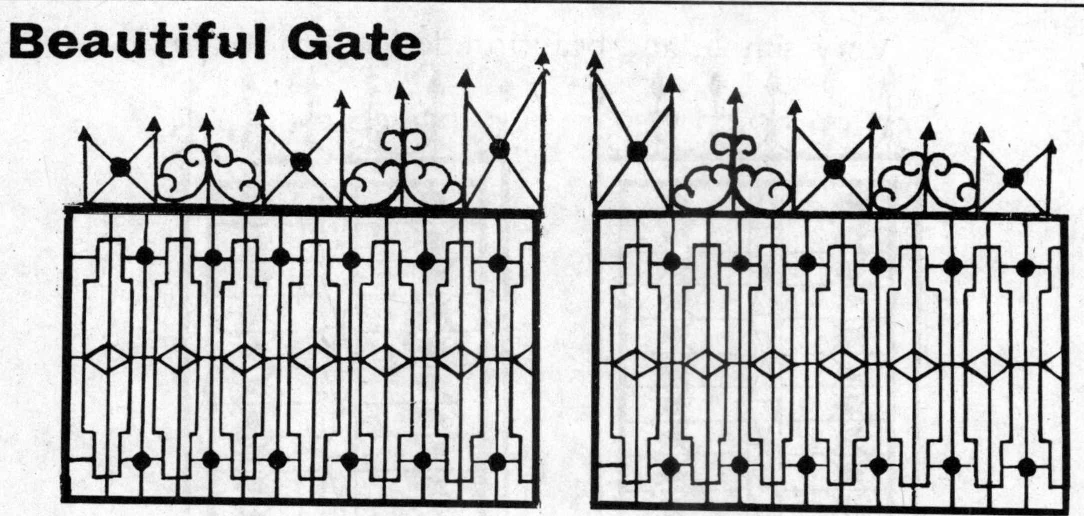

Latest design of door grills of Germany's style for Benglow, for office, College and School.

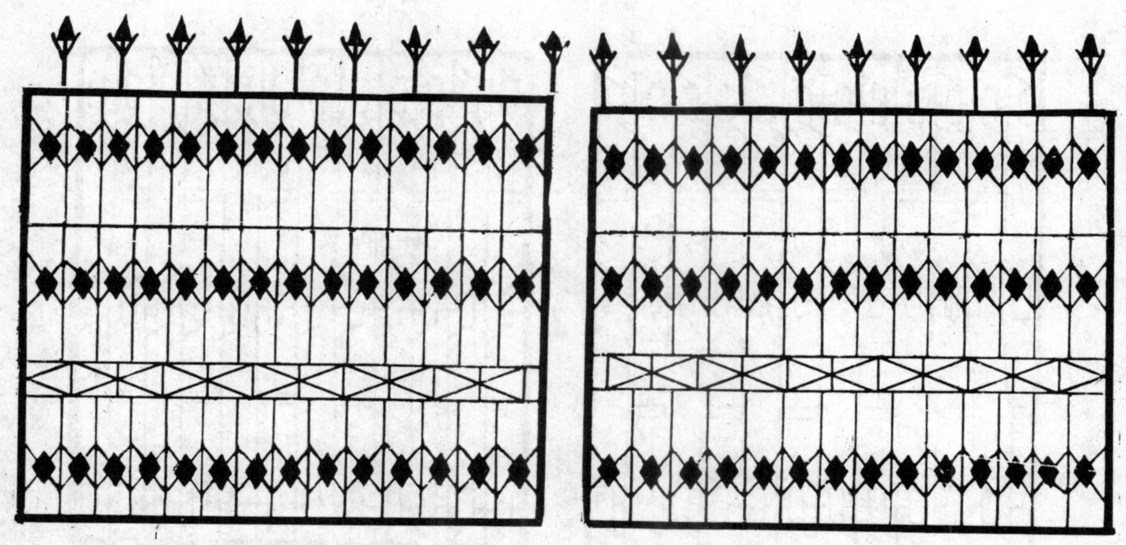

Design in Modern style is the way of modern life.

Very simple and beautiful design of Tokyo

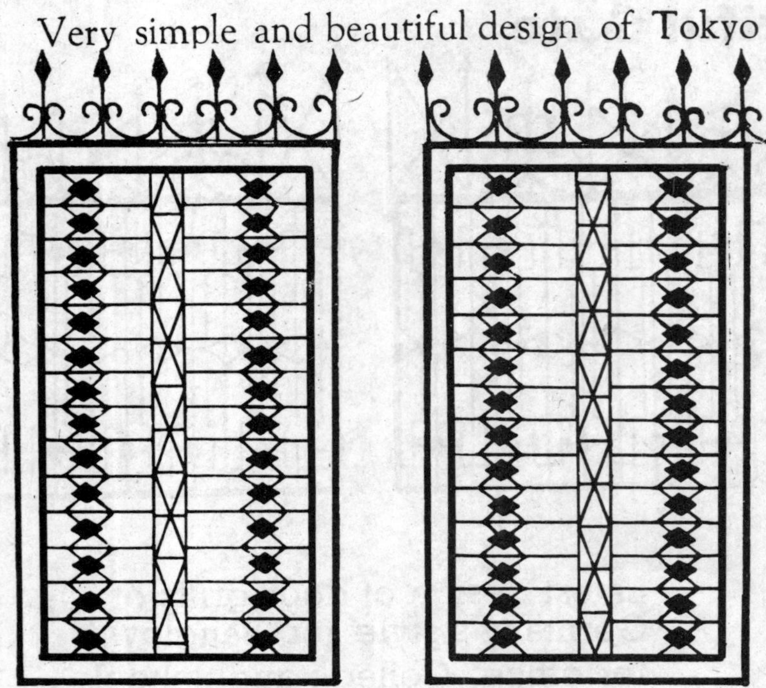

West Germany's design for biggest construction.

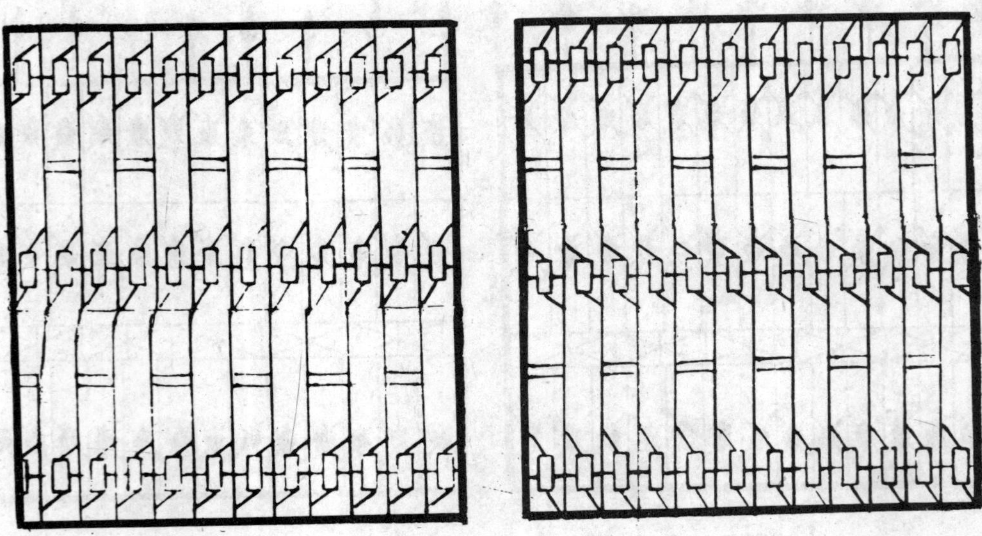

U. K. design of Gate.

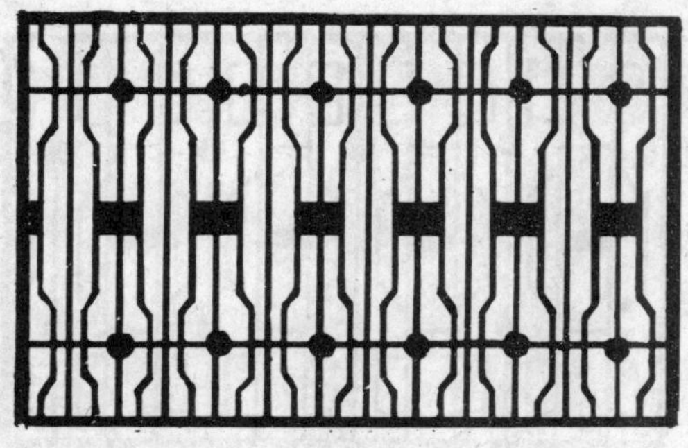
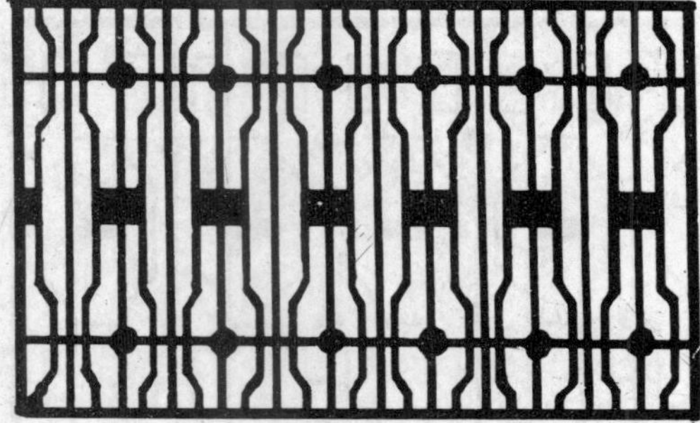

Latest German Designs, constructed with wrought Iron bars and different designs of nets

British architectural Gate Designs of Long Iron bars

Very big Gate designs. Strong and of longer life useful for

Government Offices, Schools and Colleges etc.

These designs shows the Idea
of British Ancient Art suitable
for office, College and School Buildings.

Cir. Cutting Designs of Iron bars
welded with Flate Steel Bar Frames.

Kite type design with beautiful decoration

Design of Rectangulaı frame with hanger like Top.

Best design of Gates
Made of steel sheet and thick
and thin Iron Bars.

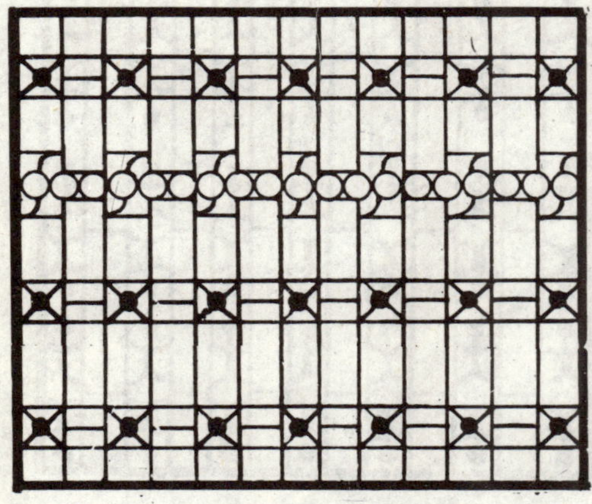

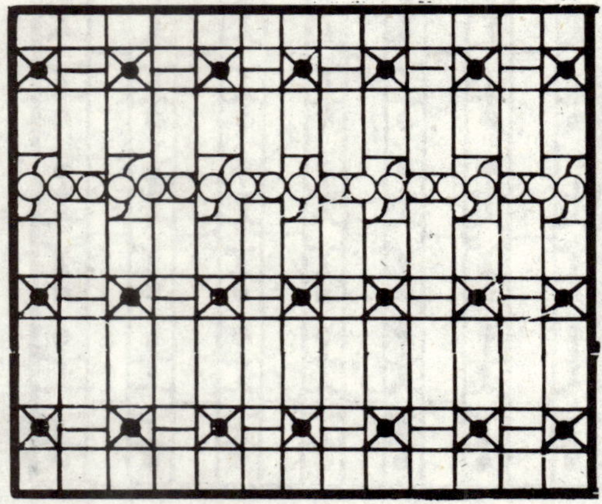

Quite Modern Big Gate design
made of steel sheet and
different nets.

Two pairs of modern designs

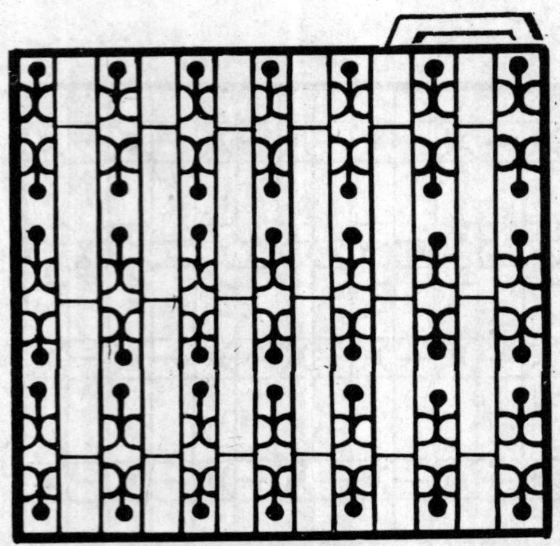

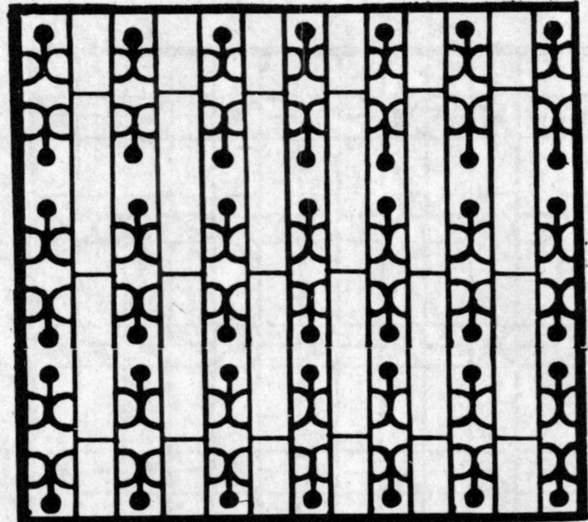

Very strong designs for decoration of residential and commercial building.

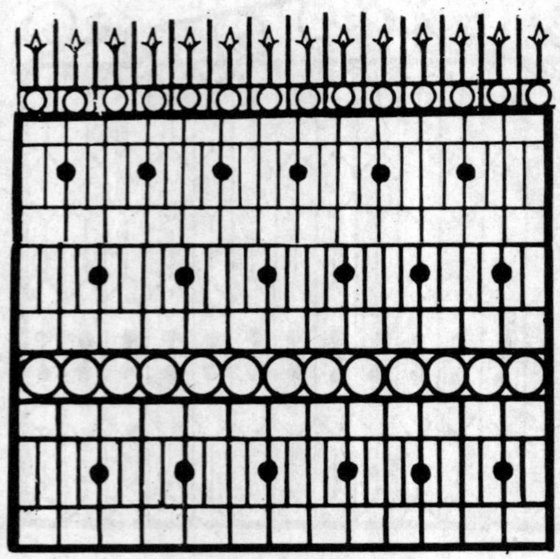

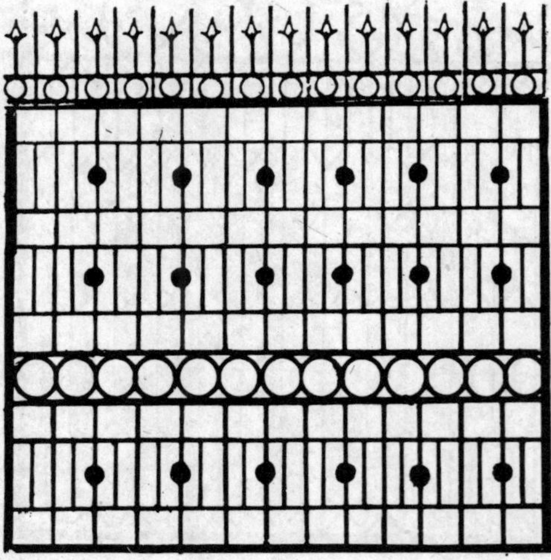

Attractive and charming design.

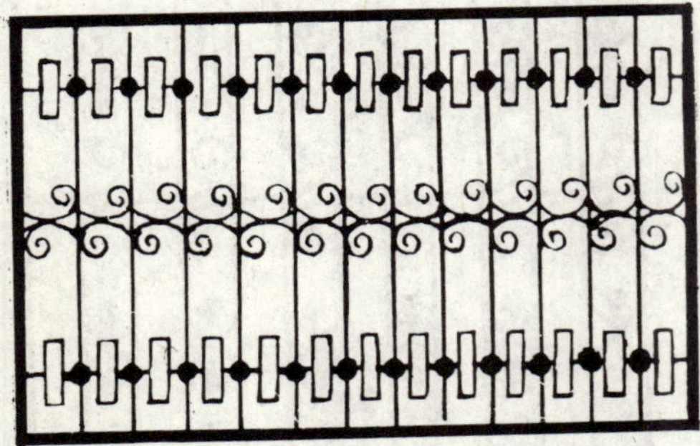
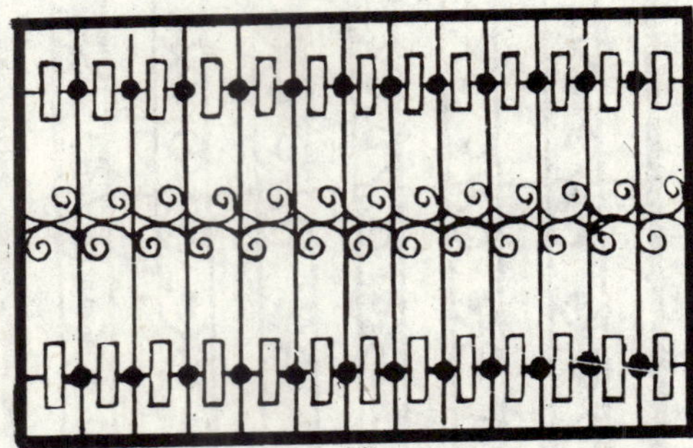

Flowery designs of solid rod and plates.

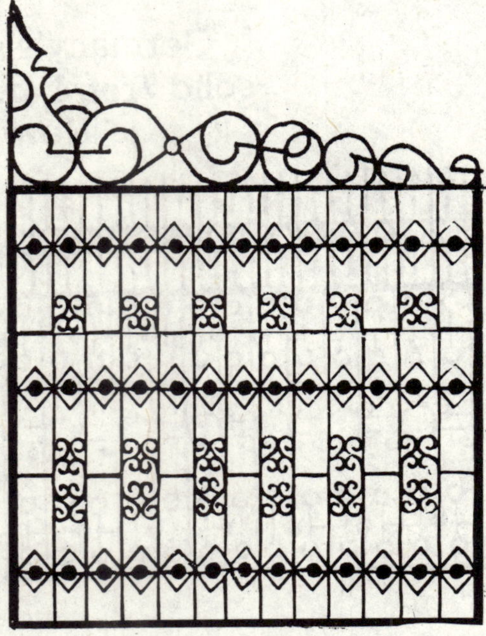

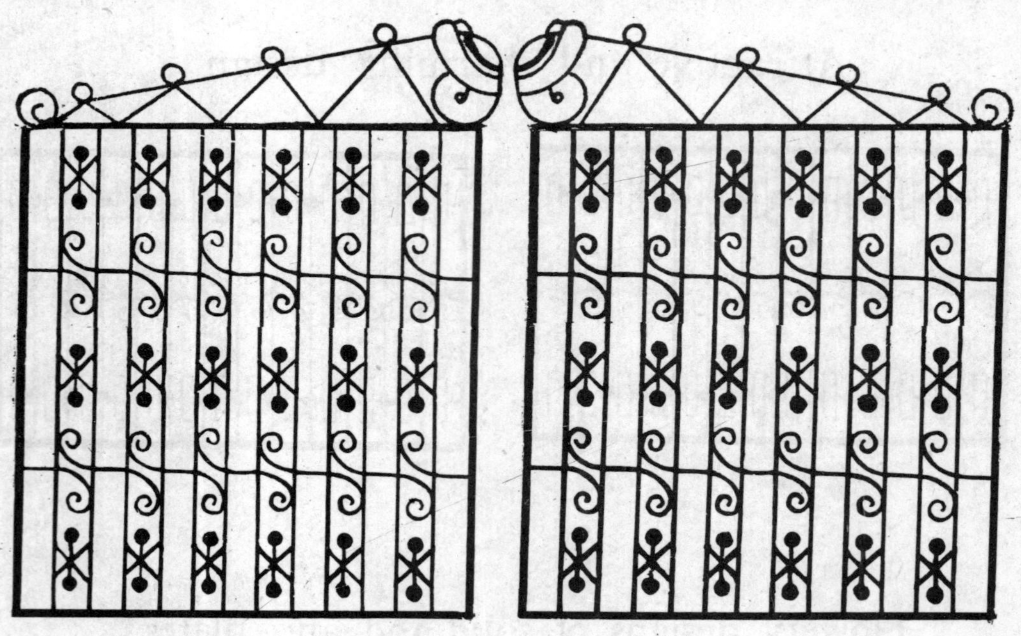

Germany's style design of
solid Iron bars of decoration for
New Building.

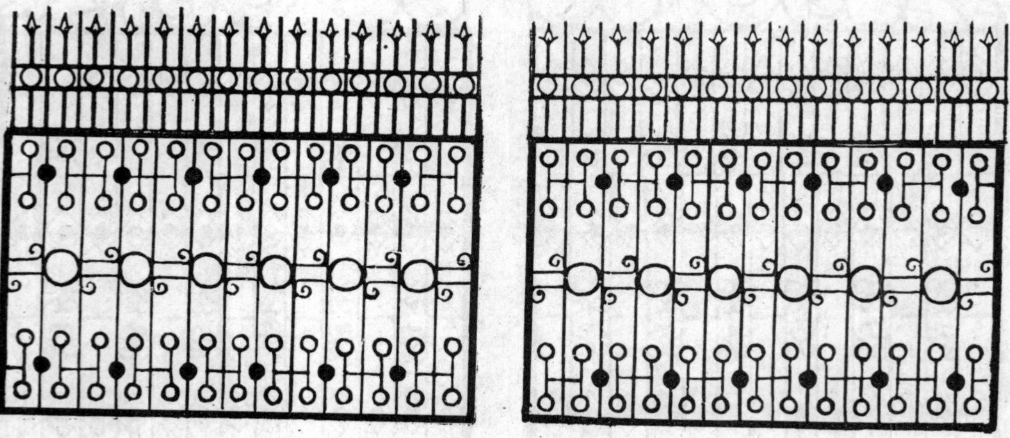

An Attractive sample of small and big circle.

Different design of iron bar in circle and harmonic curve.

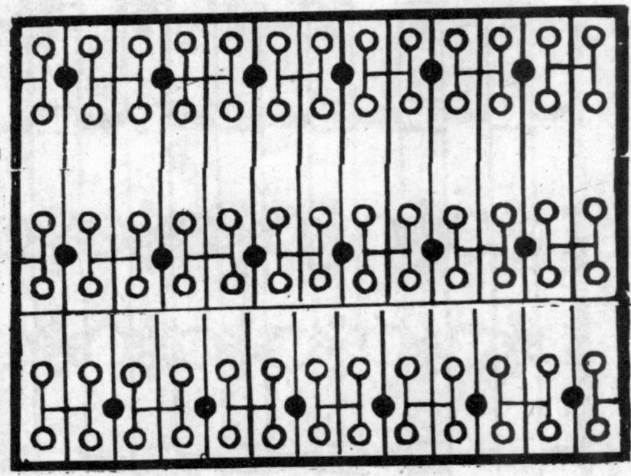

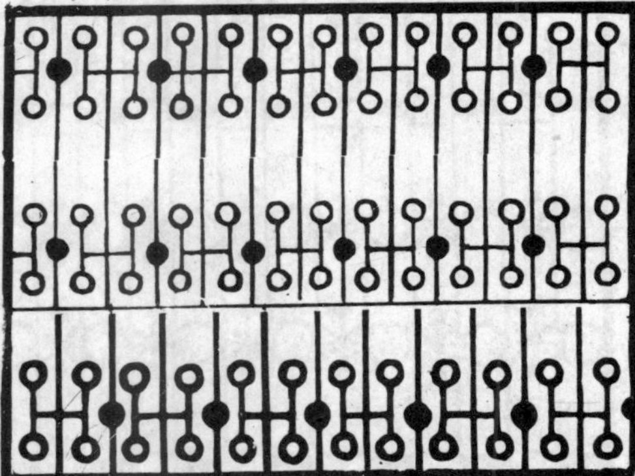

Attractive Iron Grill first designed in Germany.

Universal design for Good Building
Garden and Railway Gates etc

West Germany's design
for biggest construction.

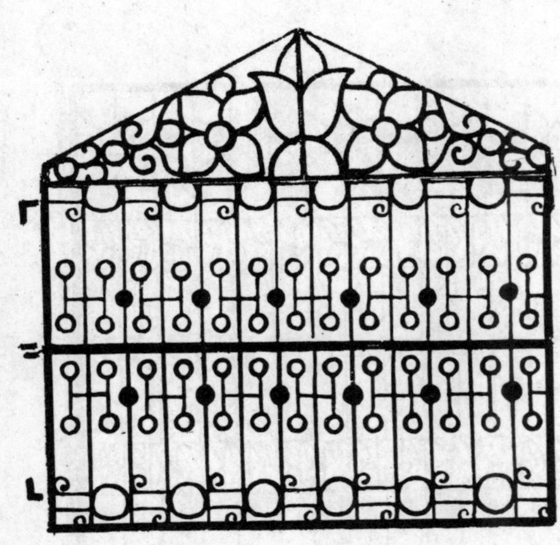
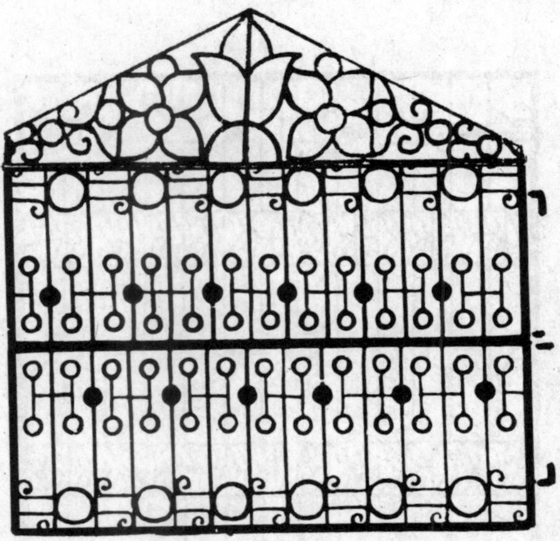

Straight Iron bar designs of Germany
solid Iron bars for Door.

Ancient Art suitable for Newly Constructed House.

New designs welded in different artistic style.

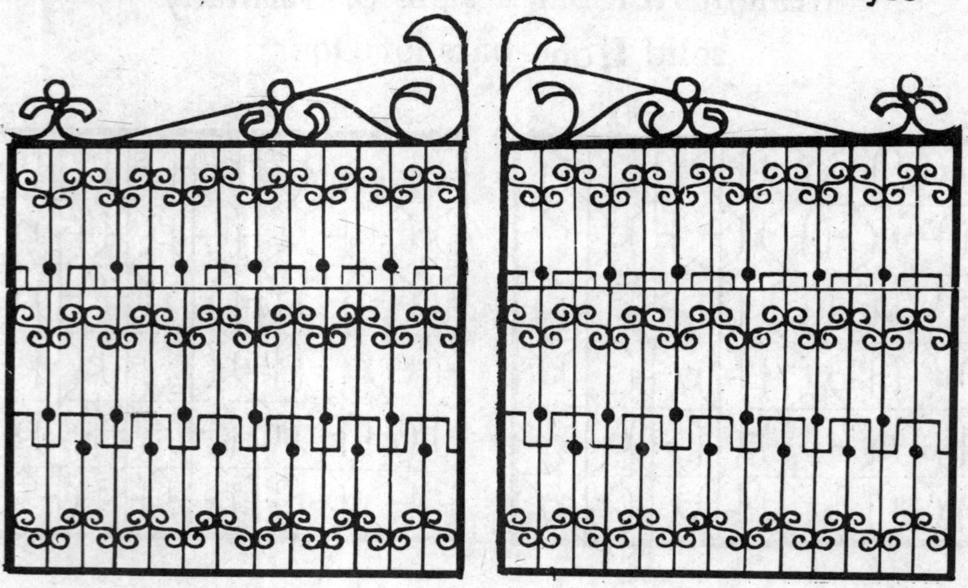

New and simple designs of penetrated Iron bars

Straight Iron bar designs of Germany

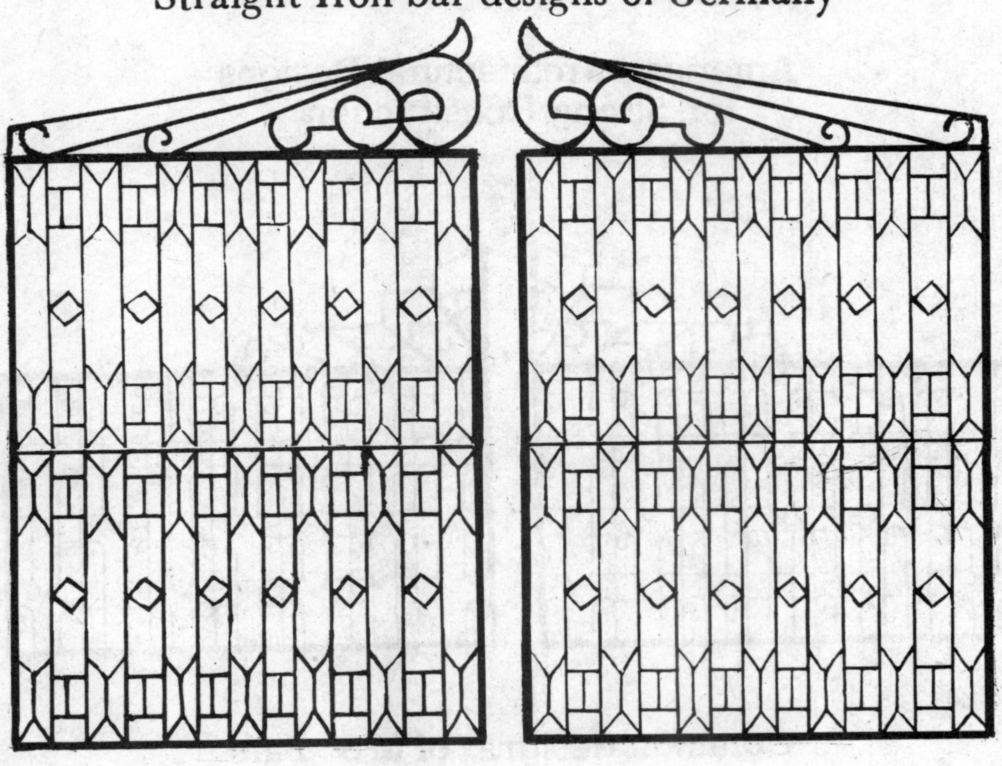

American Architectural Designs
for Strong Construction.

Common designs of M.S Bars
Quite suitable for Low Cost Houses.

British architectural Gate Designs of Long Iron bars

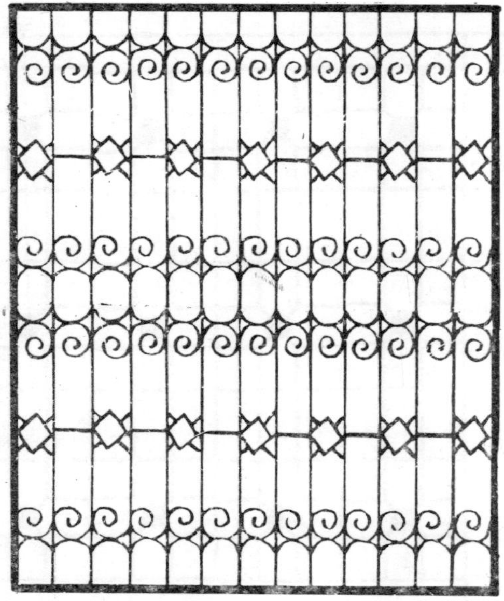

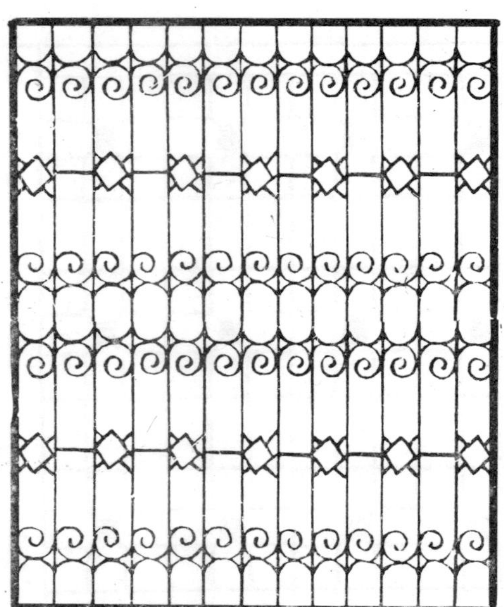

Decorative Poland Style designs of Railing and doors.

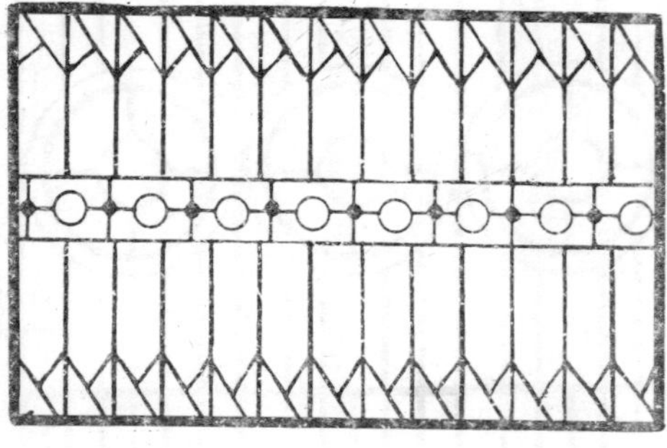

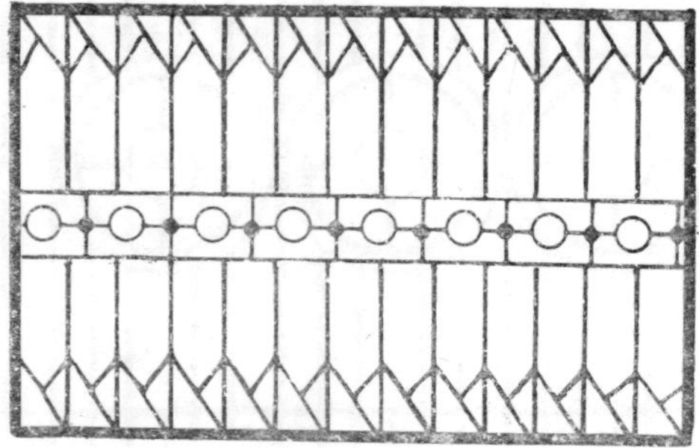

Latest Designs of straight welded with pipes, for Big Embassy.

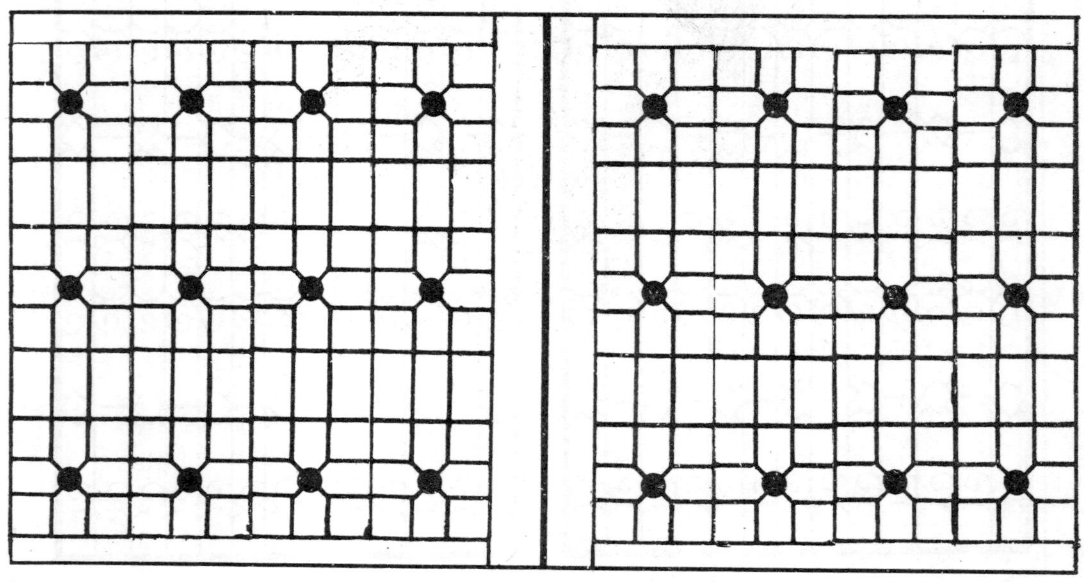

West Germany's Designs for New Decoration.

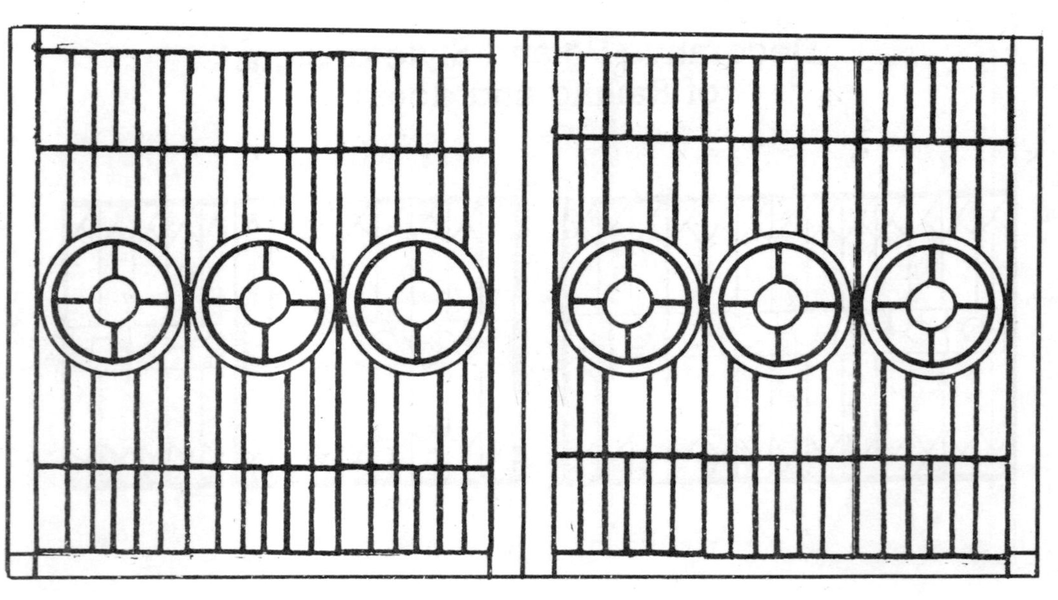

Charming design of leaves and rings for modernity.

Modern Design based on Architectural construction.

Design of 'Stars welded and inserted with Iron bars

Artistic Design of Cost Iron Rod and curve's

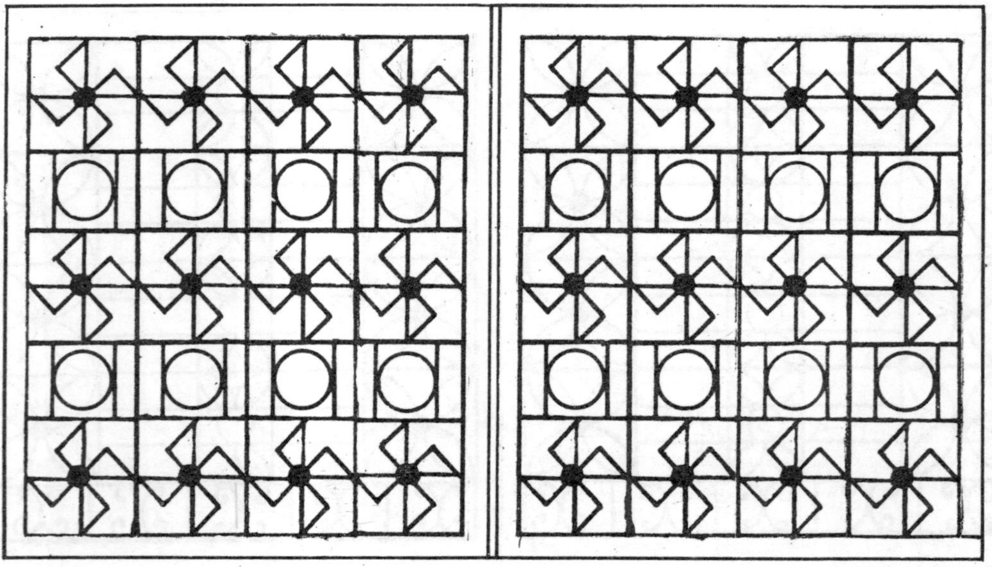

A composition of latest design with different style of Rectangular Iron bar

Gate

Flowery design of wrought Iron bars,

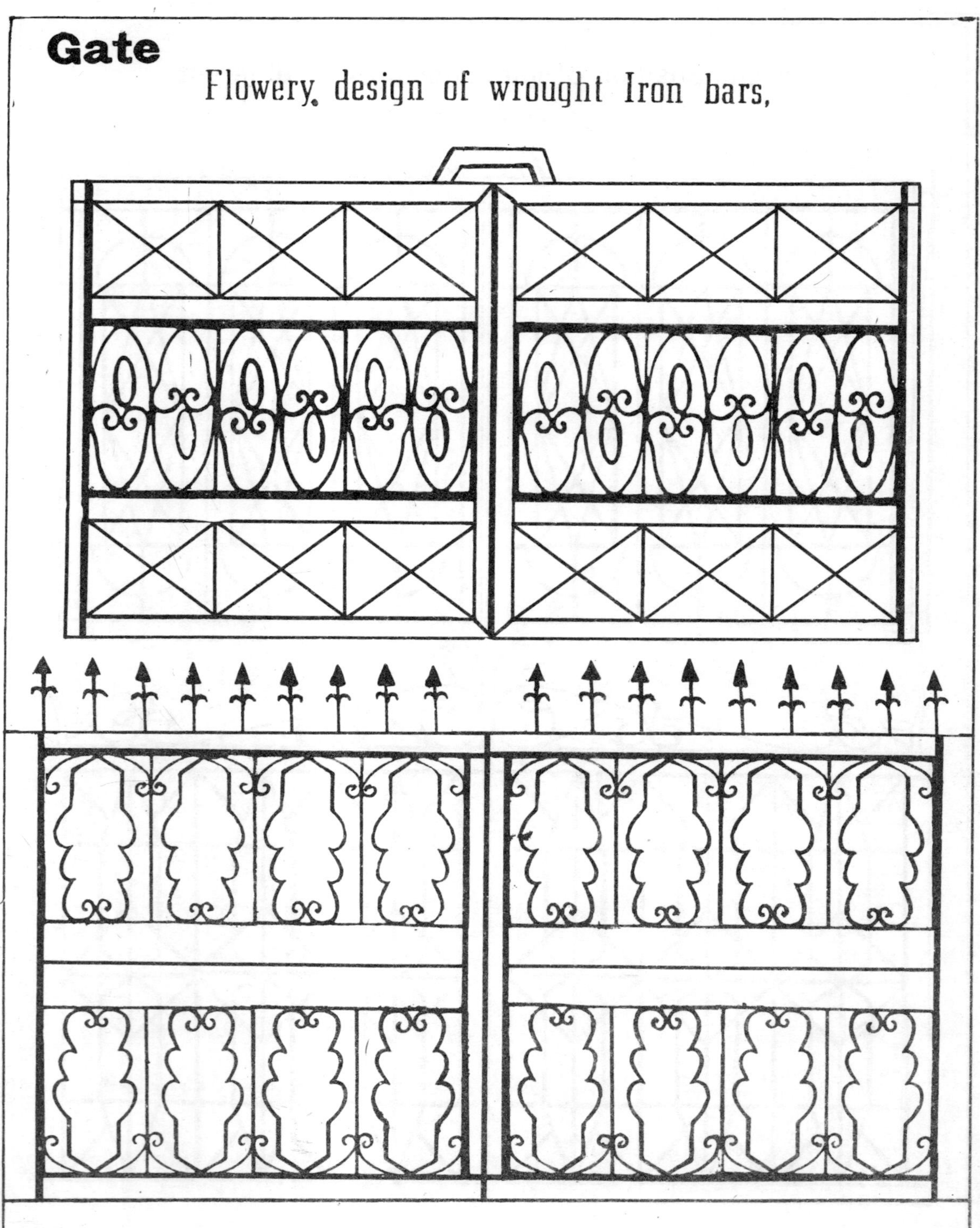

Modern design of door grills of Germany's style.

Ultra-modern designs of thick and thin solid road welded in Geometrical principle.

Architectural design of solid Square bar frame.

Attractive Modern Designs based on Folk Art.

Artistic and Charming Sunflower design of famous Indian style for Strong Construction.

Beautiful Gate

Art of Mughal Period

Latest design of solid Iron bars in square and circular style

Art of Mughal Period Designs

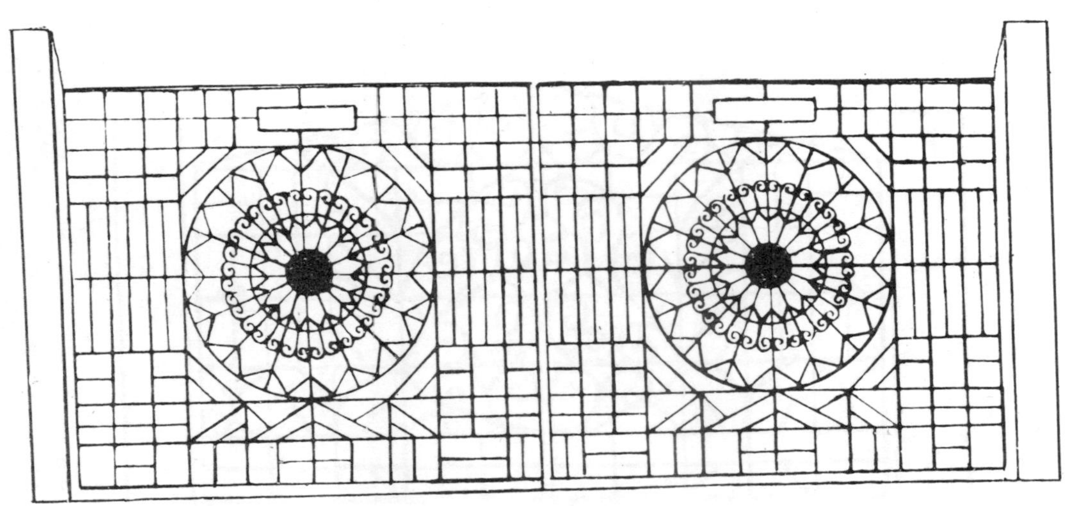

This complete design gives idea and art of the Mughal period.

Very Good design for Archological Building.

British architectural Gate Designs of Long Iron bars

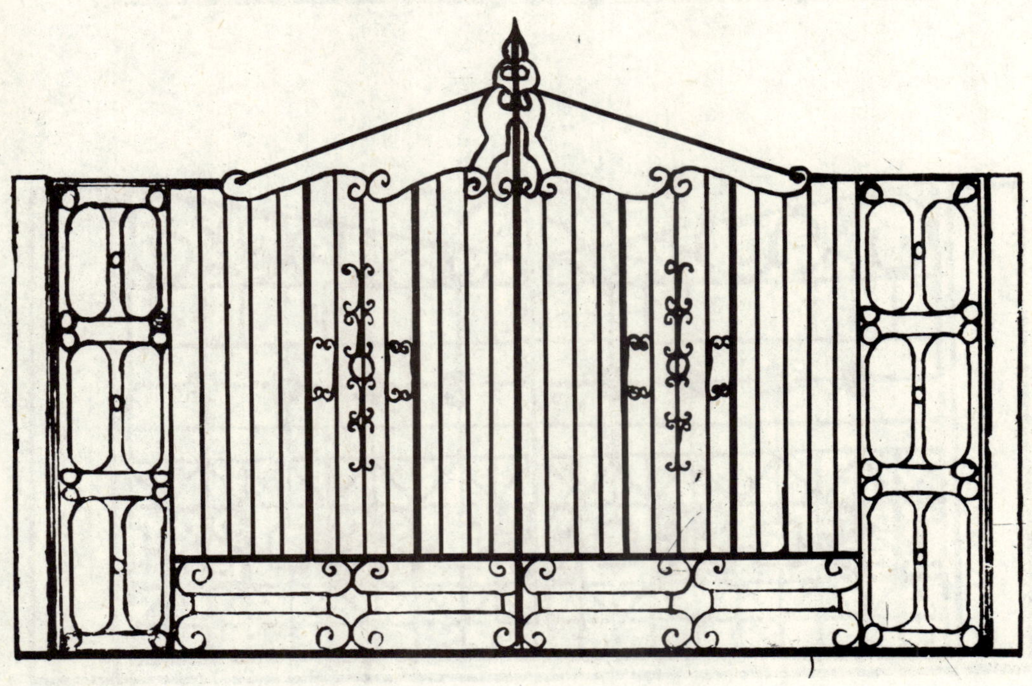

A composition of
Best and latest design of modern style.

Gats and Grilles

Five Japanese designs for new Bunglow.

A Common design of Gates for Small and Big Factories.

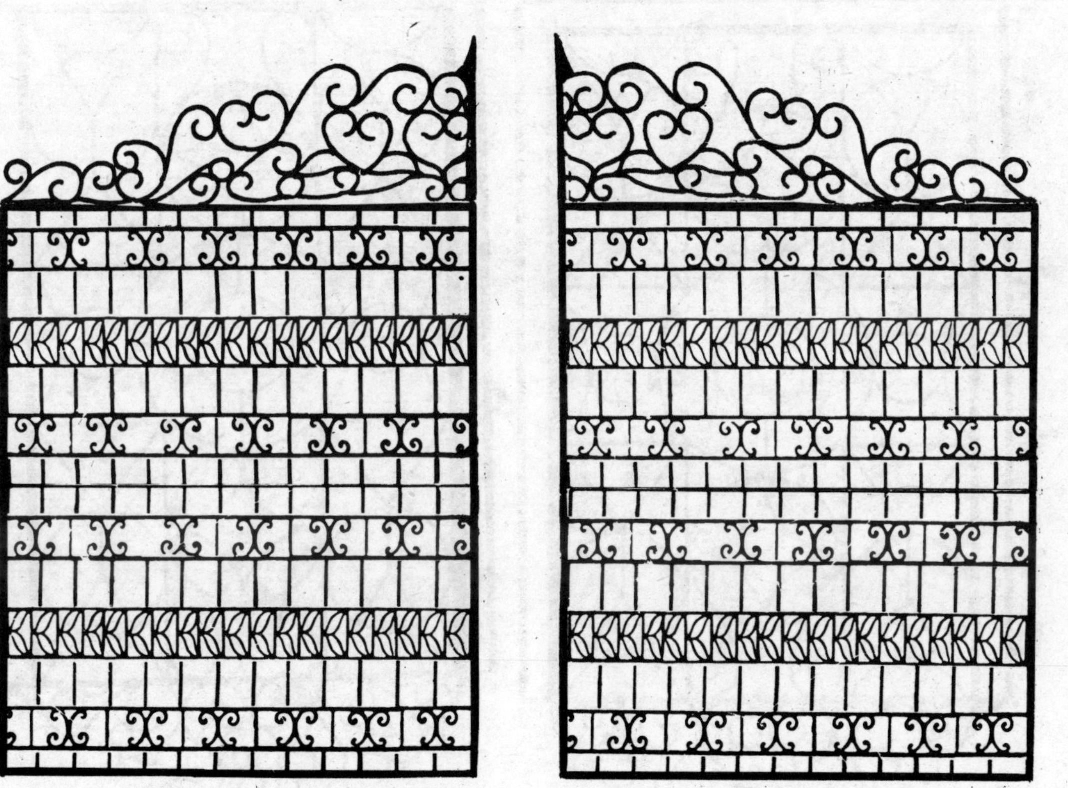

Latest design of door grills of Ancient Art decoration for well Planned Building.

British Ancient Art suitable for well Planned Building.

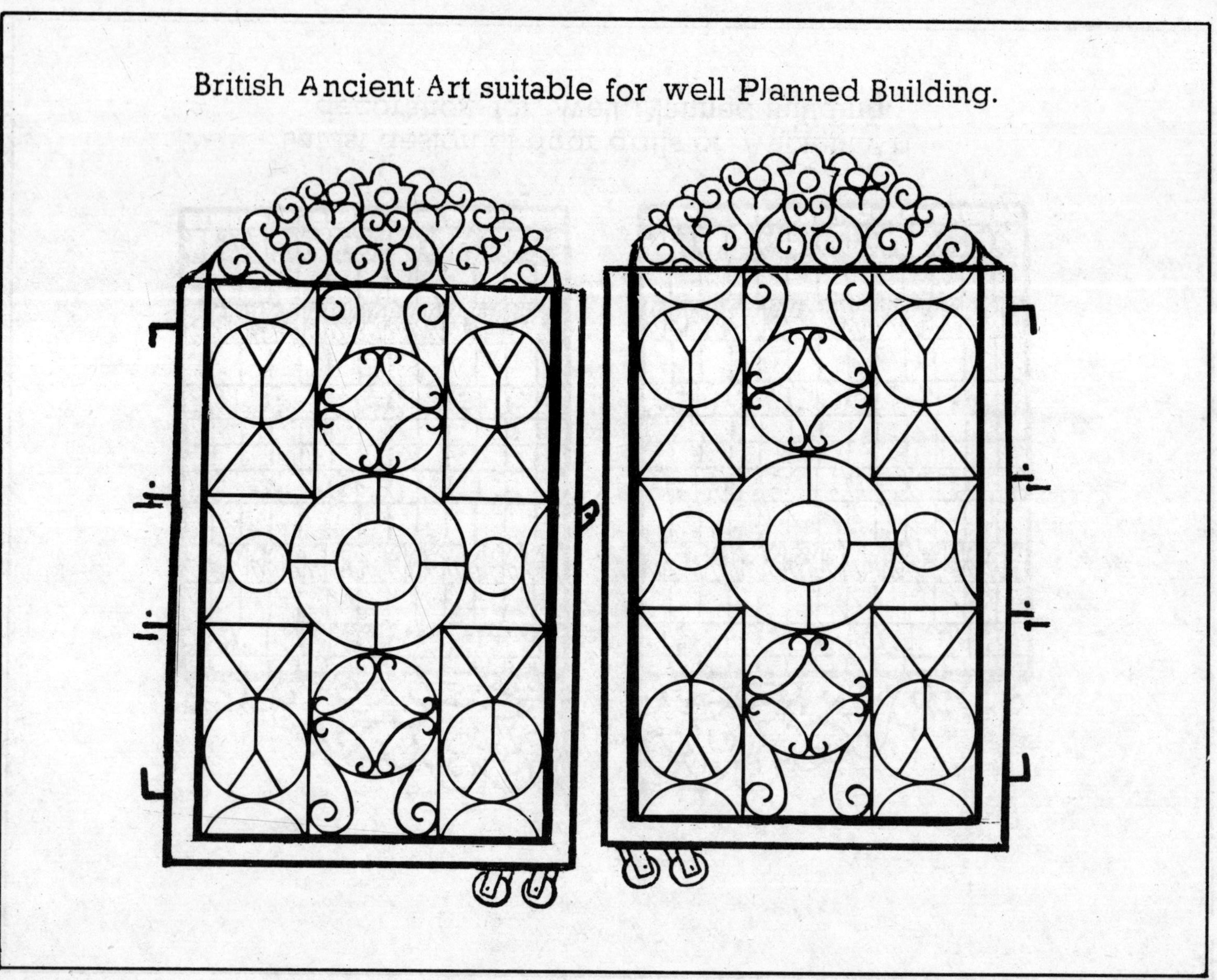

Ultramodern designs of Poland.

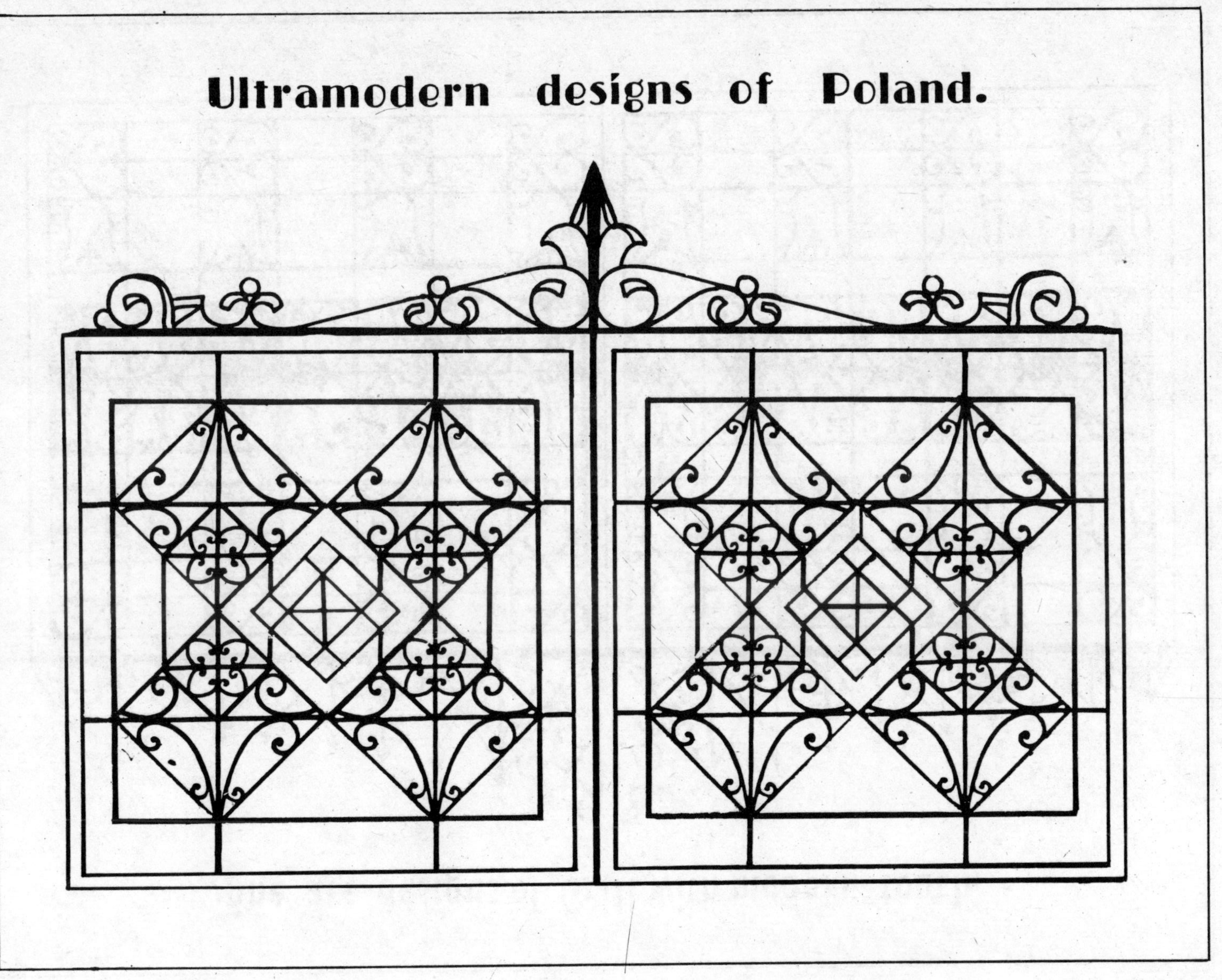

fine art designs of Grill with modern touch.

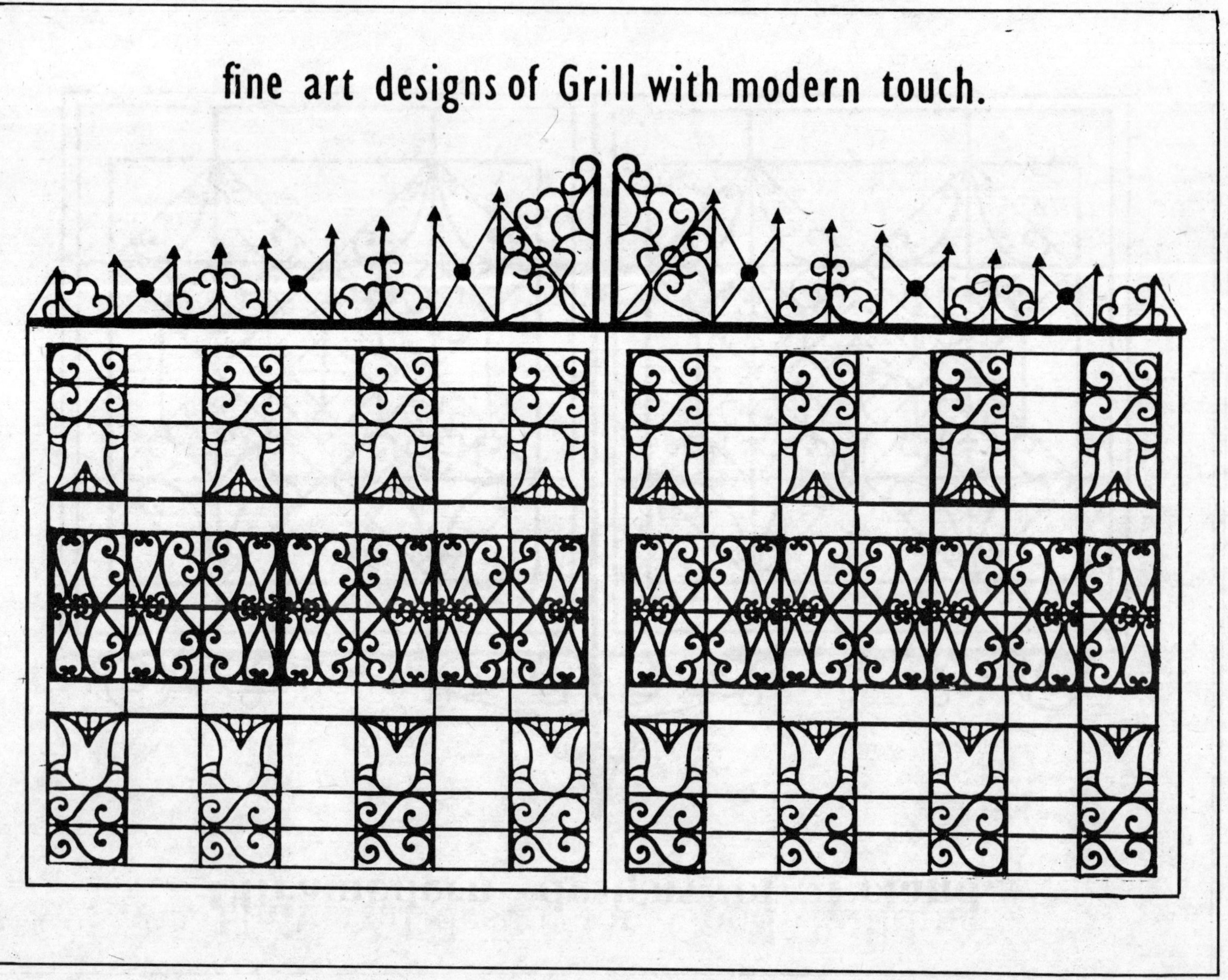

Universal design for Good Building

Japanese designs for Railway Gate

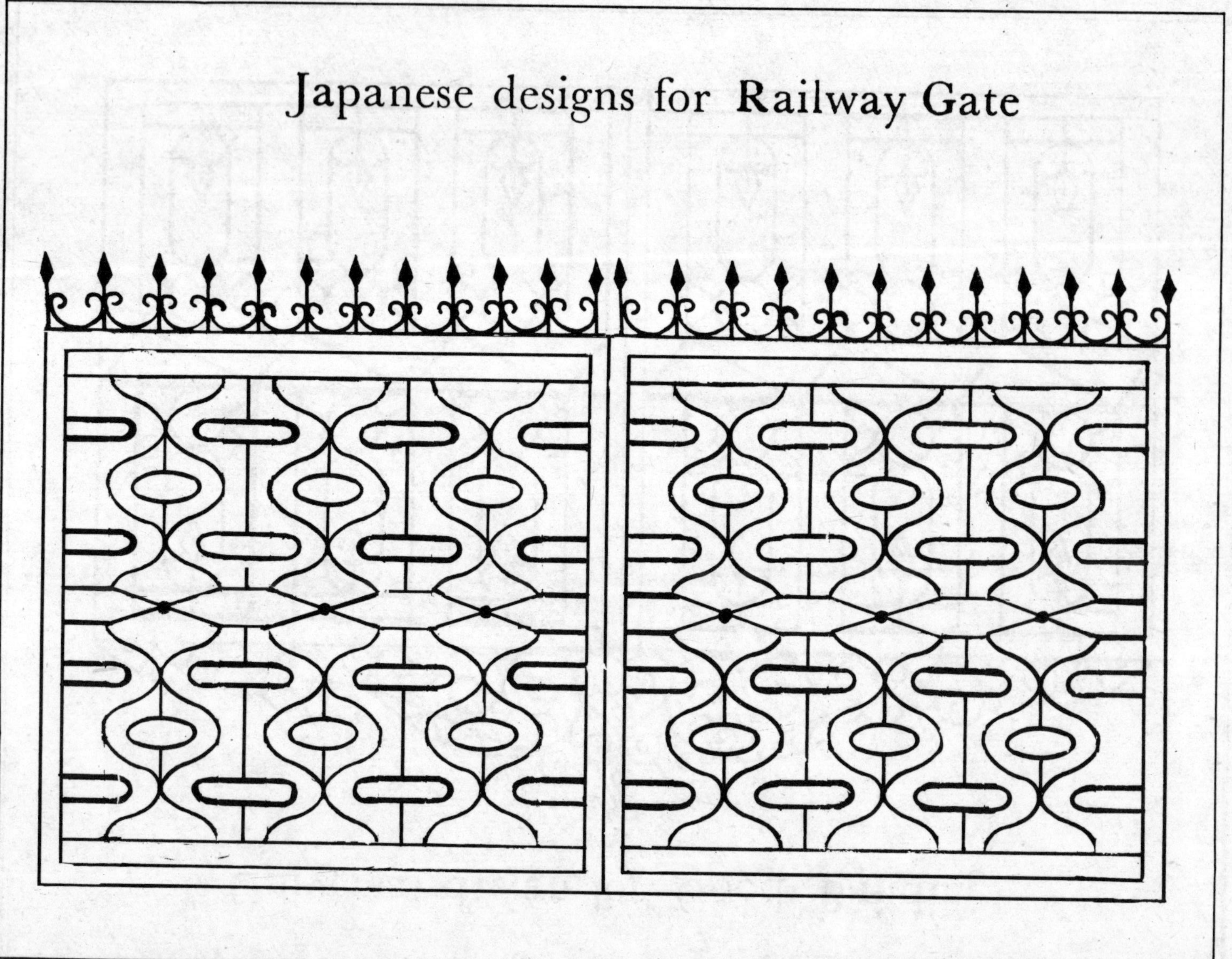

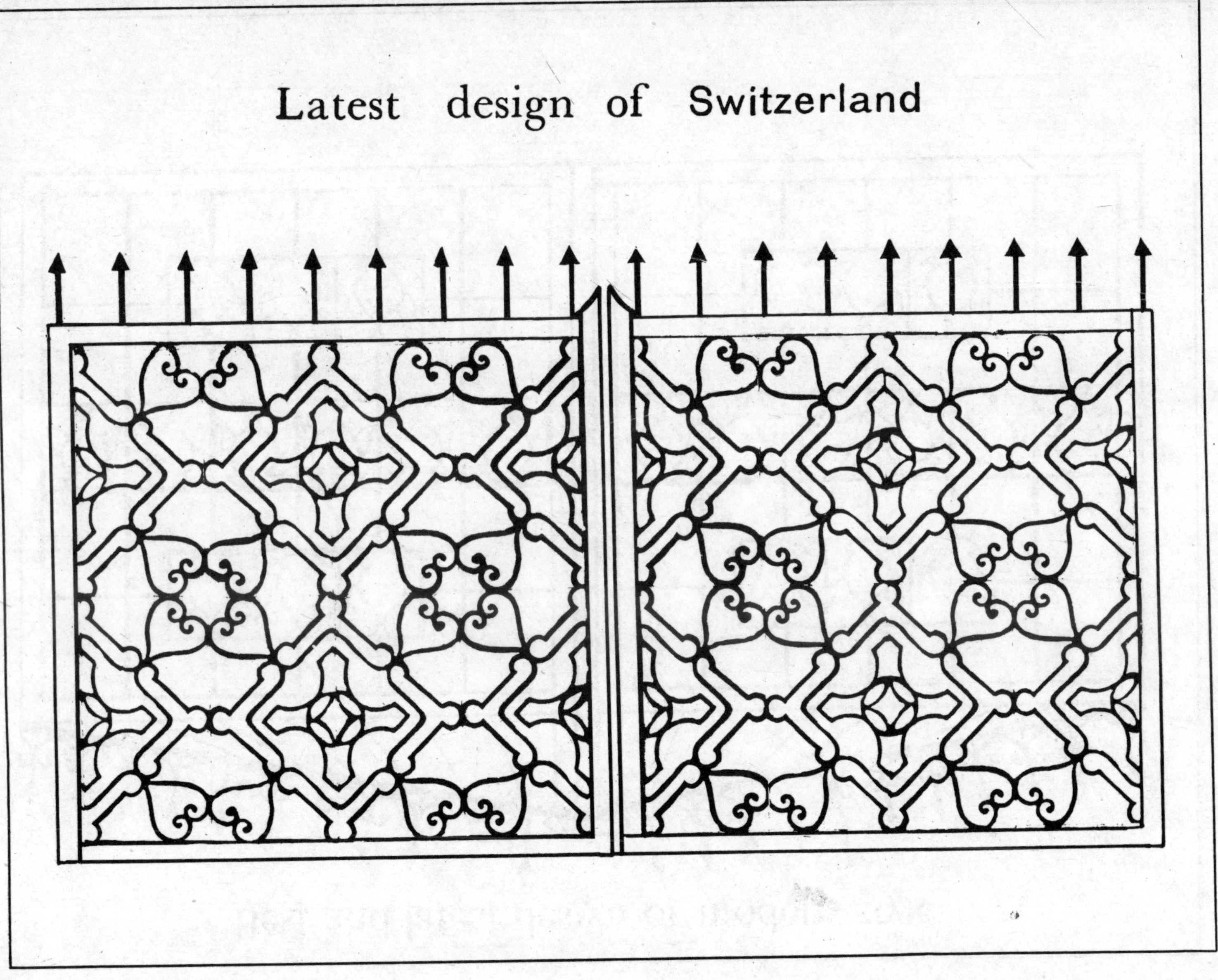

Latest design of Switzerland

Best and latest design of modern style.

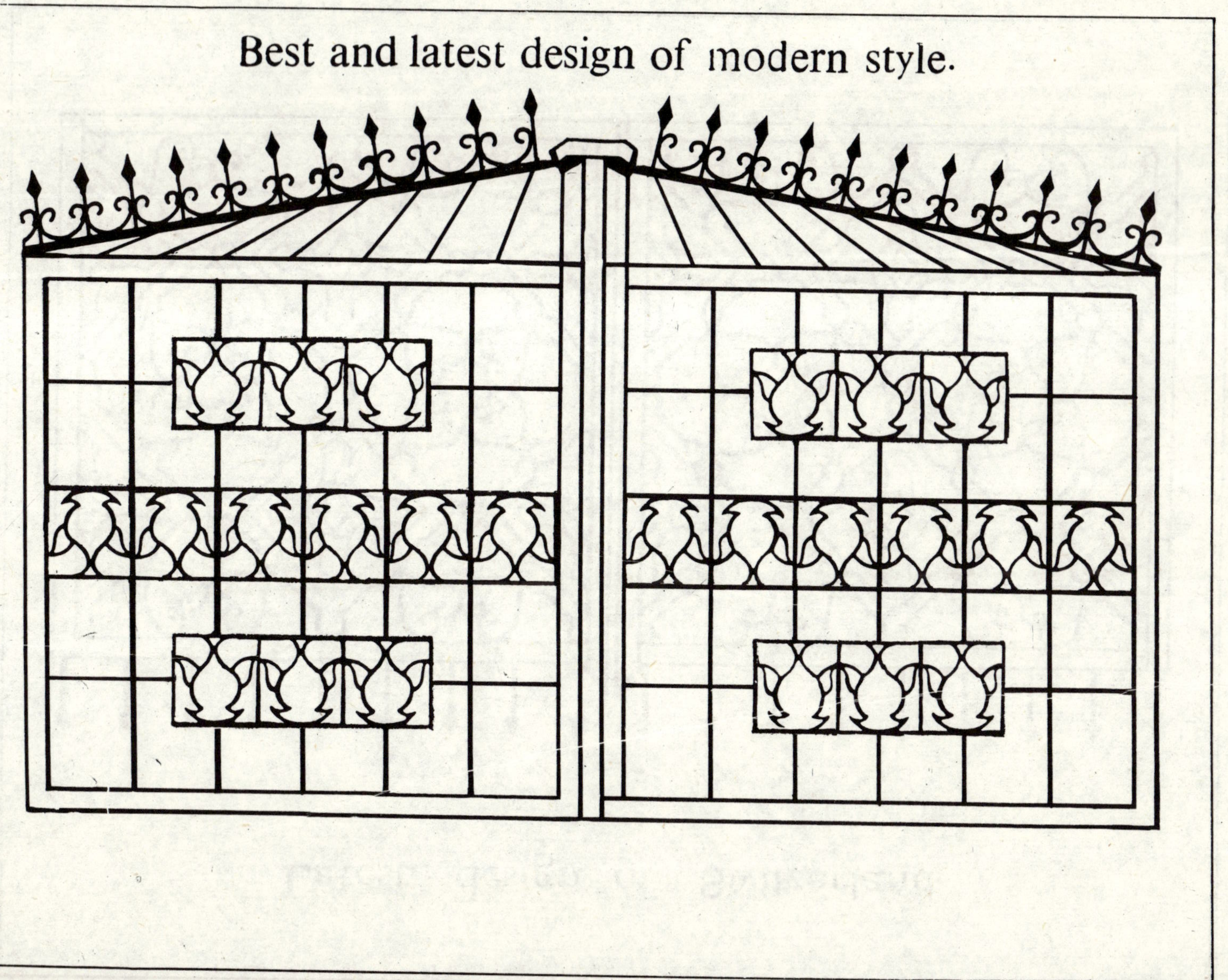

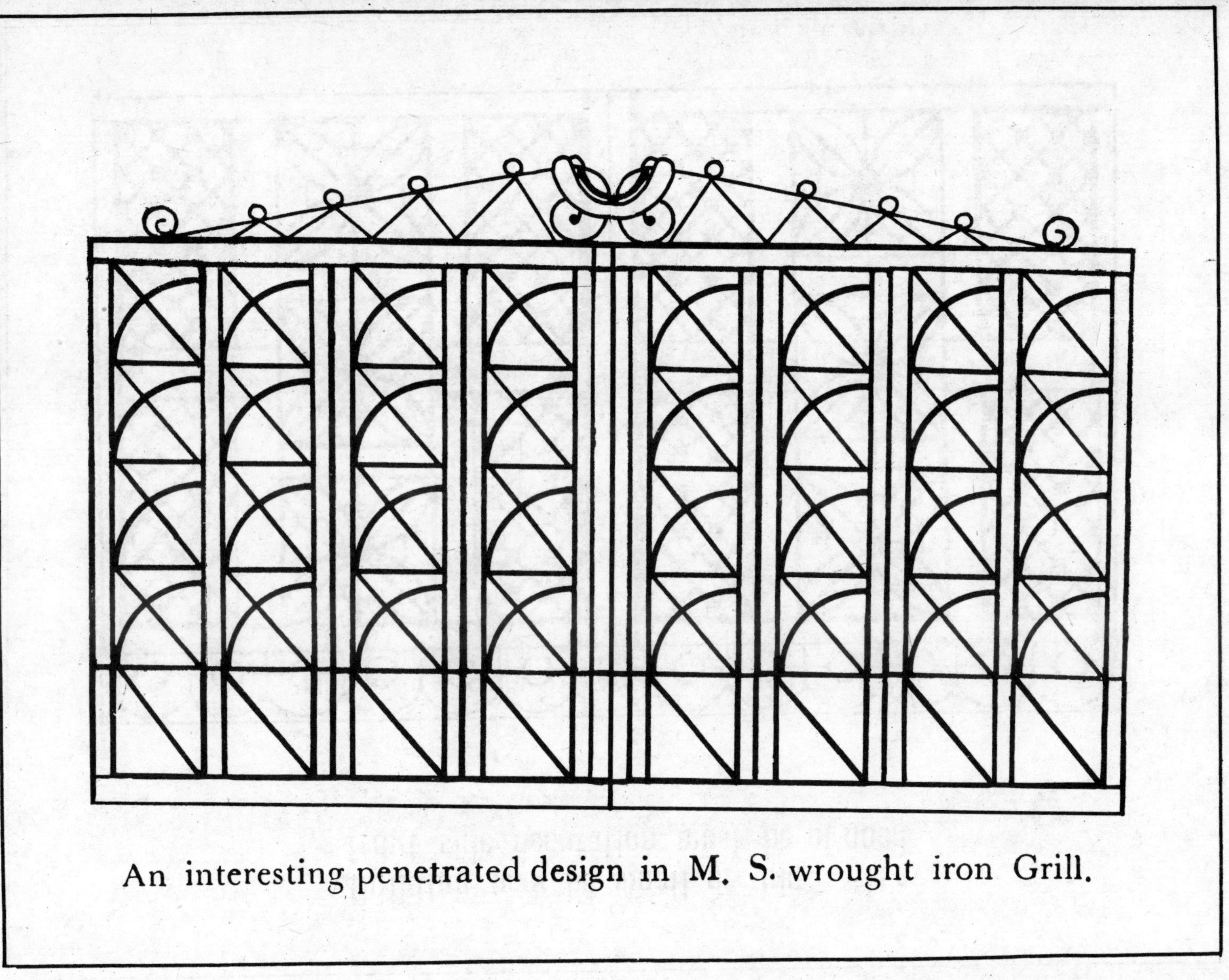

An interesting penetrated design in M. S. wrought iron Grill.

Building mav be small or big. It's front side decoration must be of good

Very beautiful designs of modern decoration.

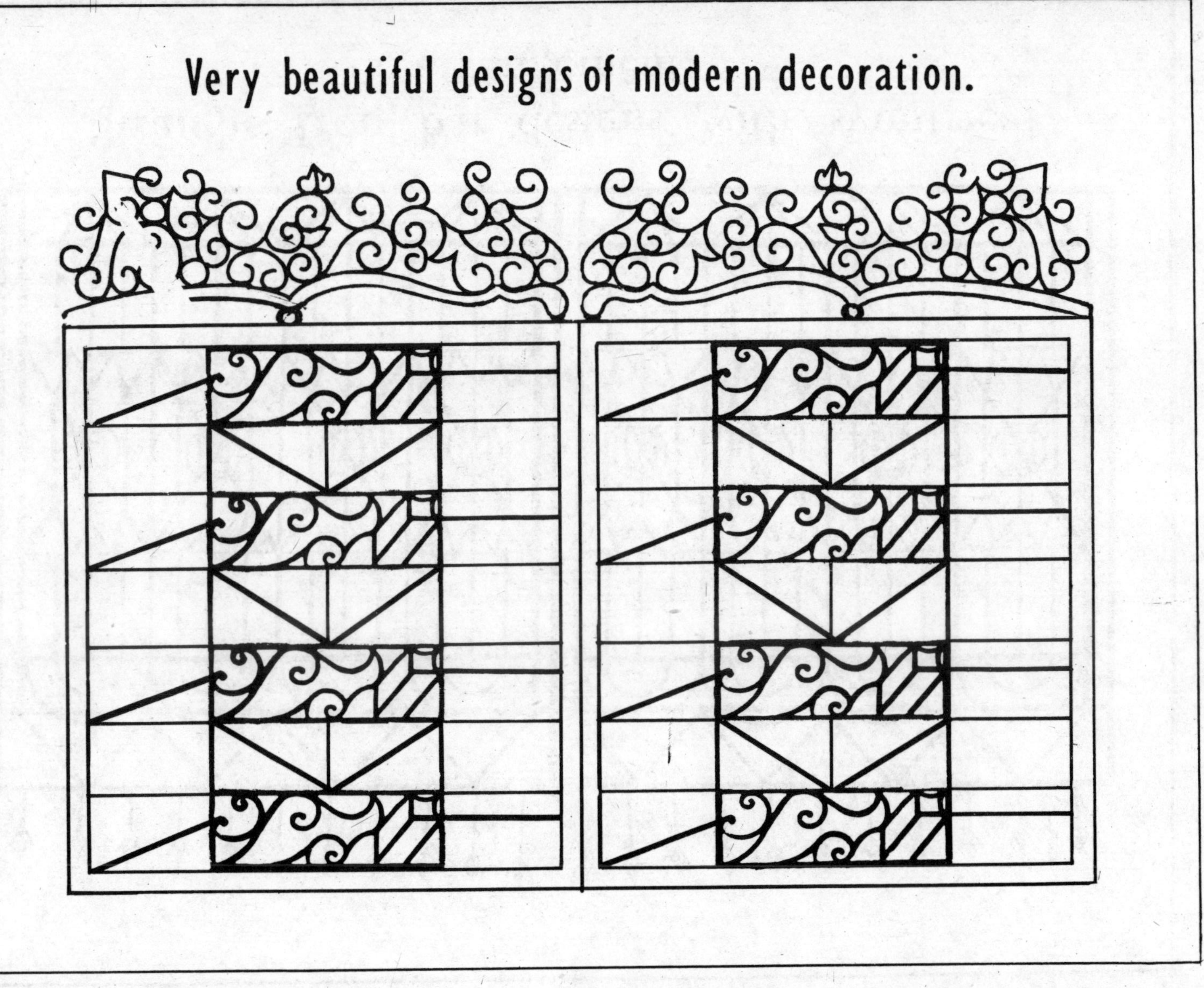

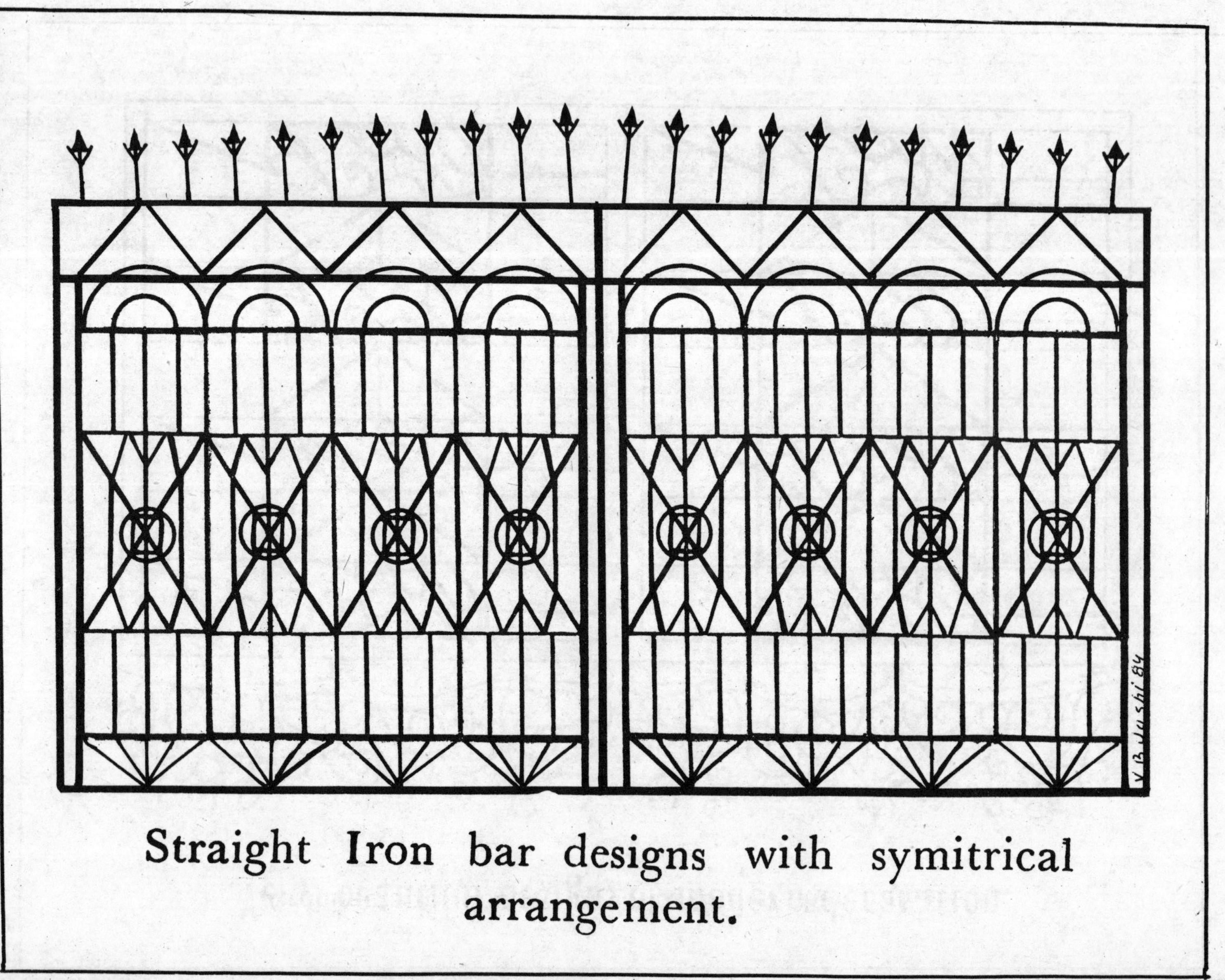

Straight Iron bar designs with symitrical arrangement.

Architectural design of solid Square bar frame.

Architectural designs for modern construction and decoration

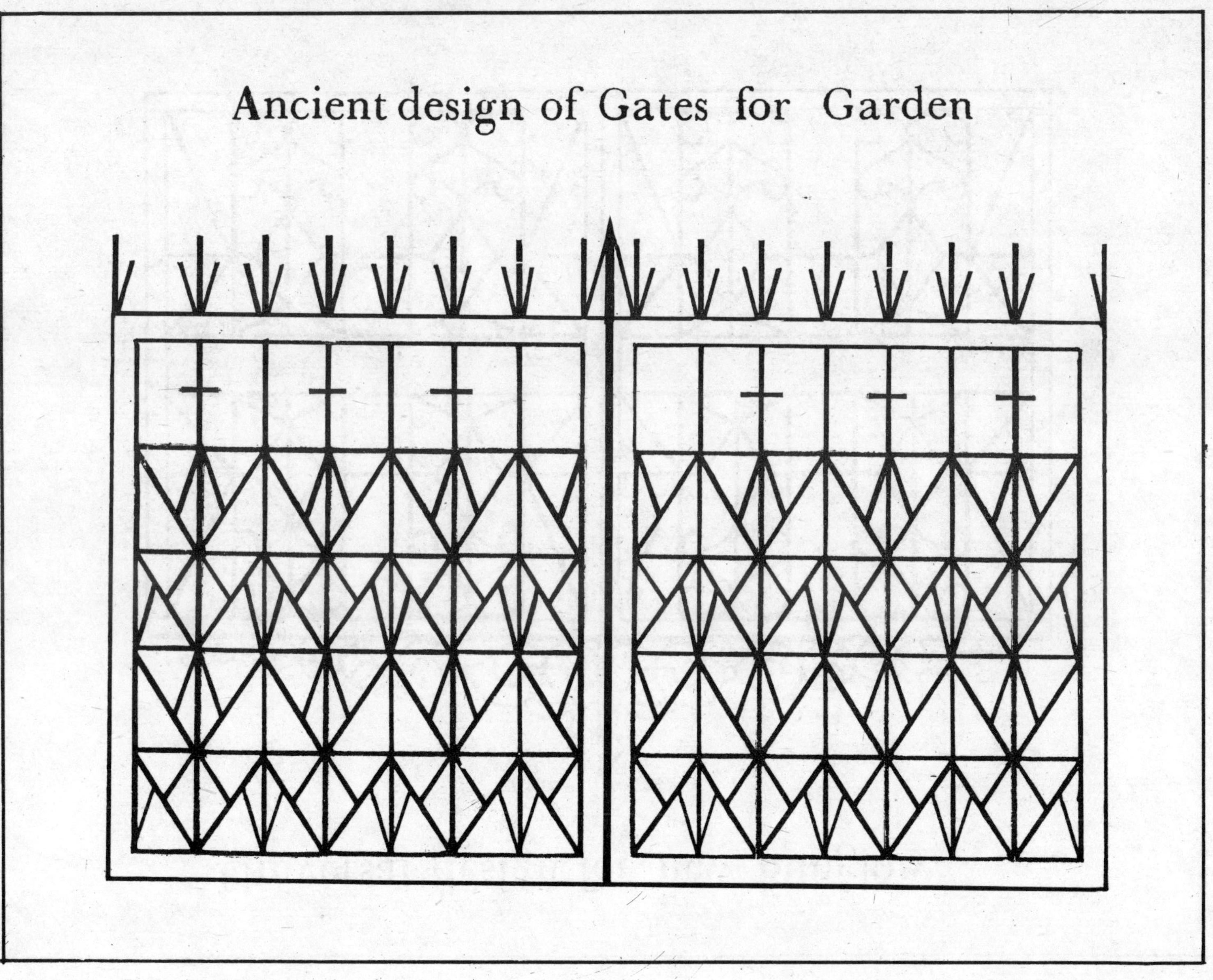

Ancient design of Gates for Garden

Universal design for new **Bunglow.**

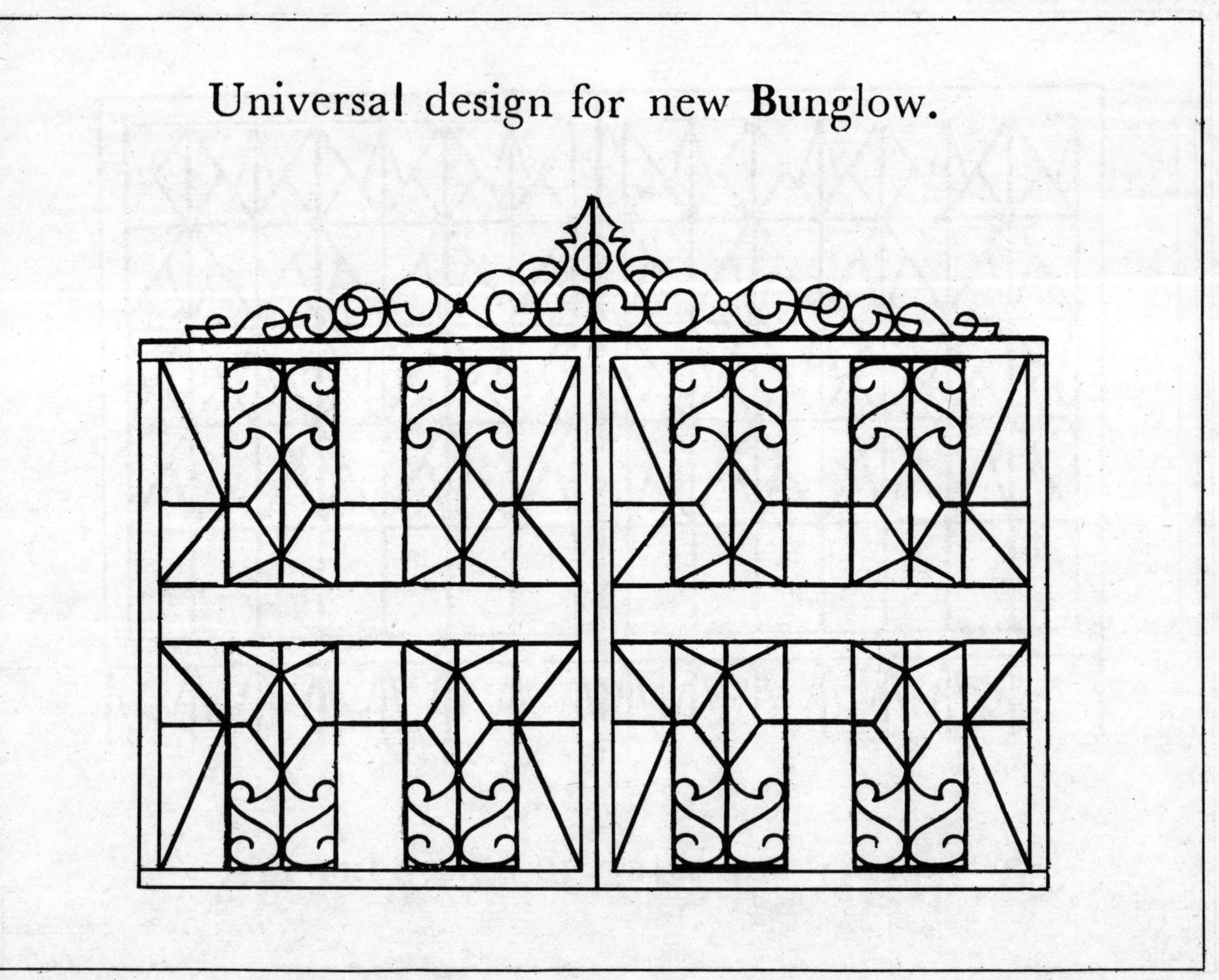

Iron bars curved in Indian folk art design.

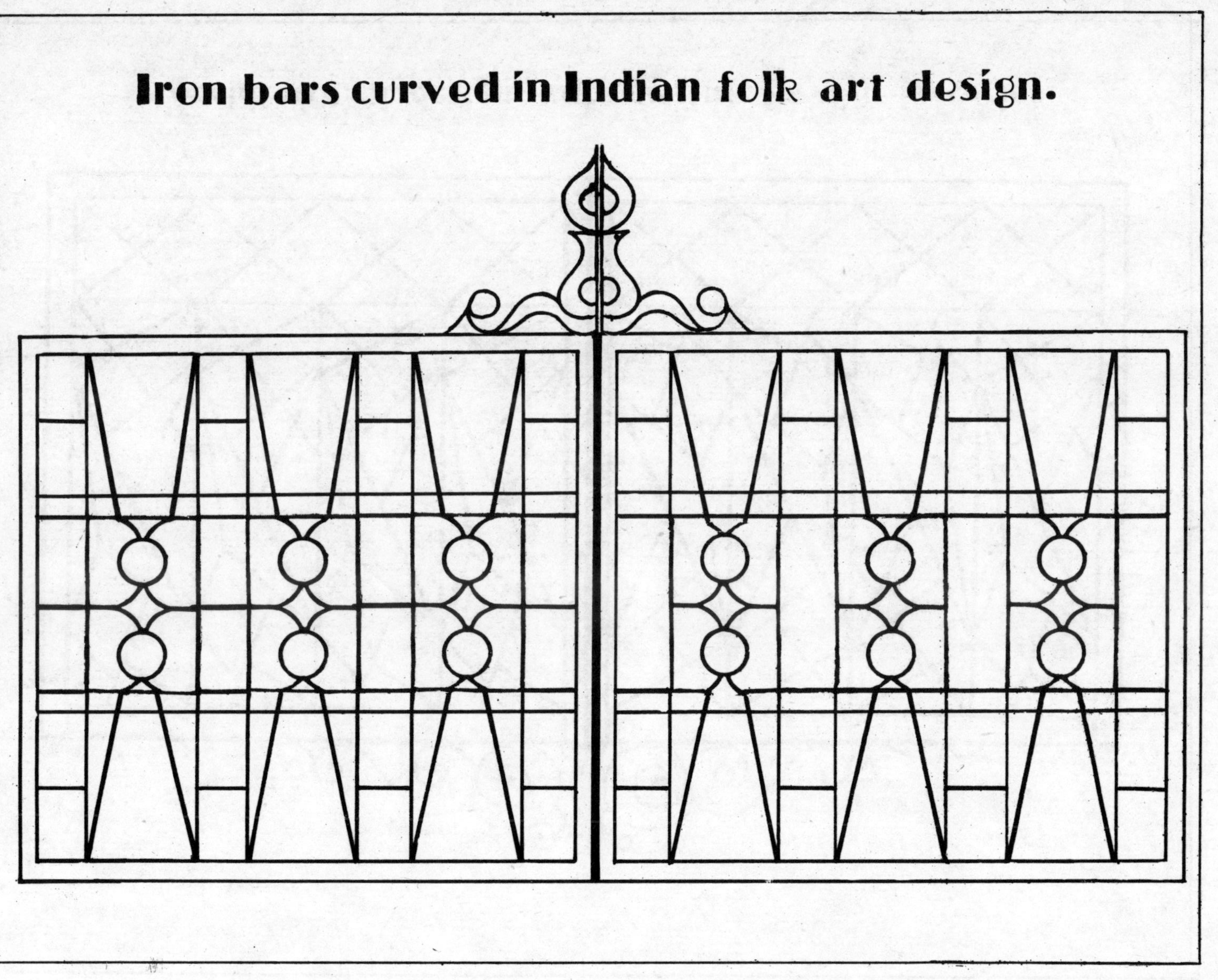

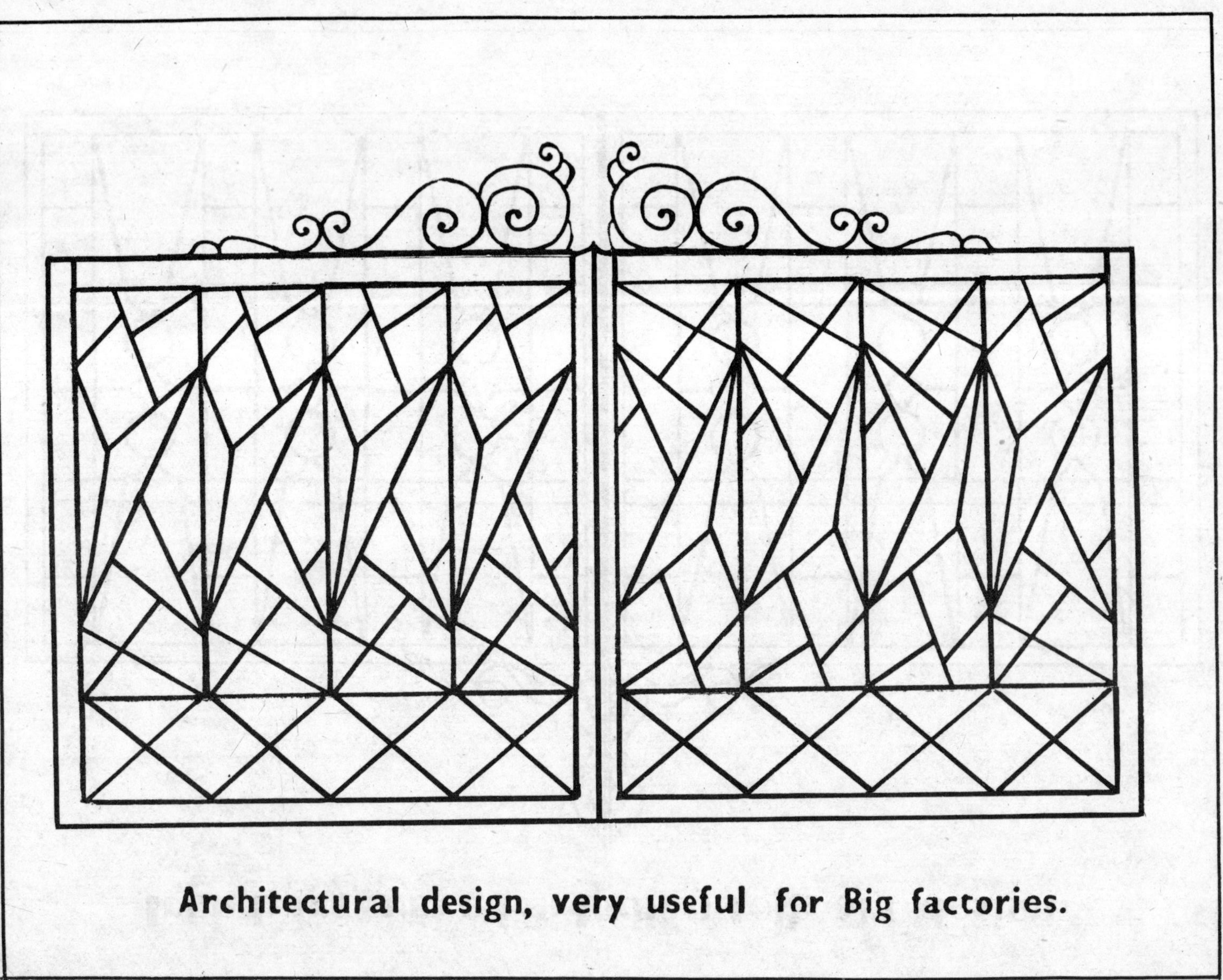

Architectural design, very useful for Big factories.

Universal design for Good Building

Most attractive fine art design in wrought iron bars construction

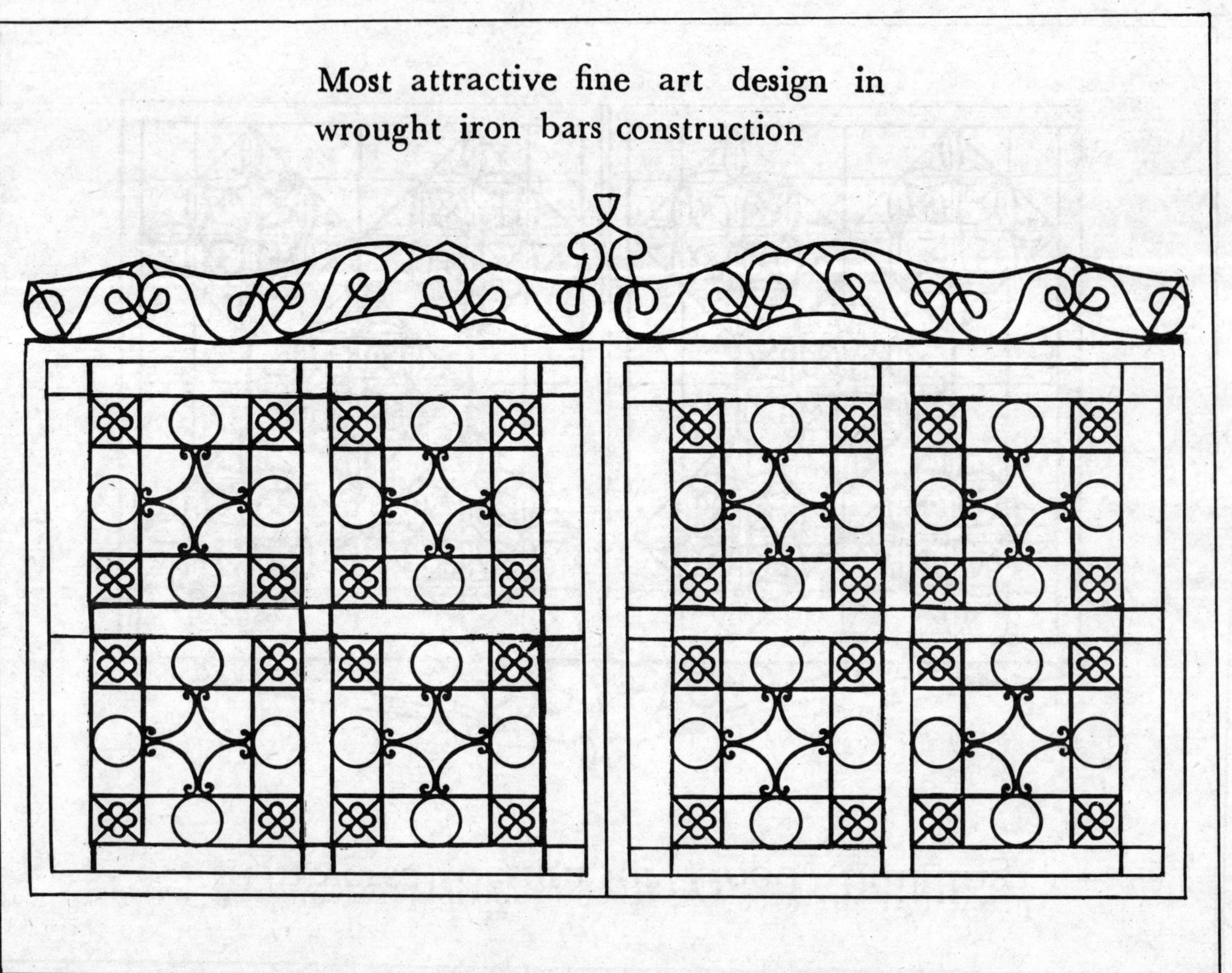

Architectural designs in M. S. wrought iron Grill.

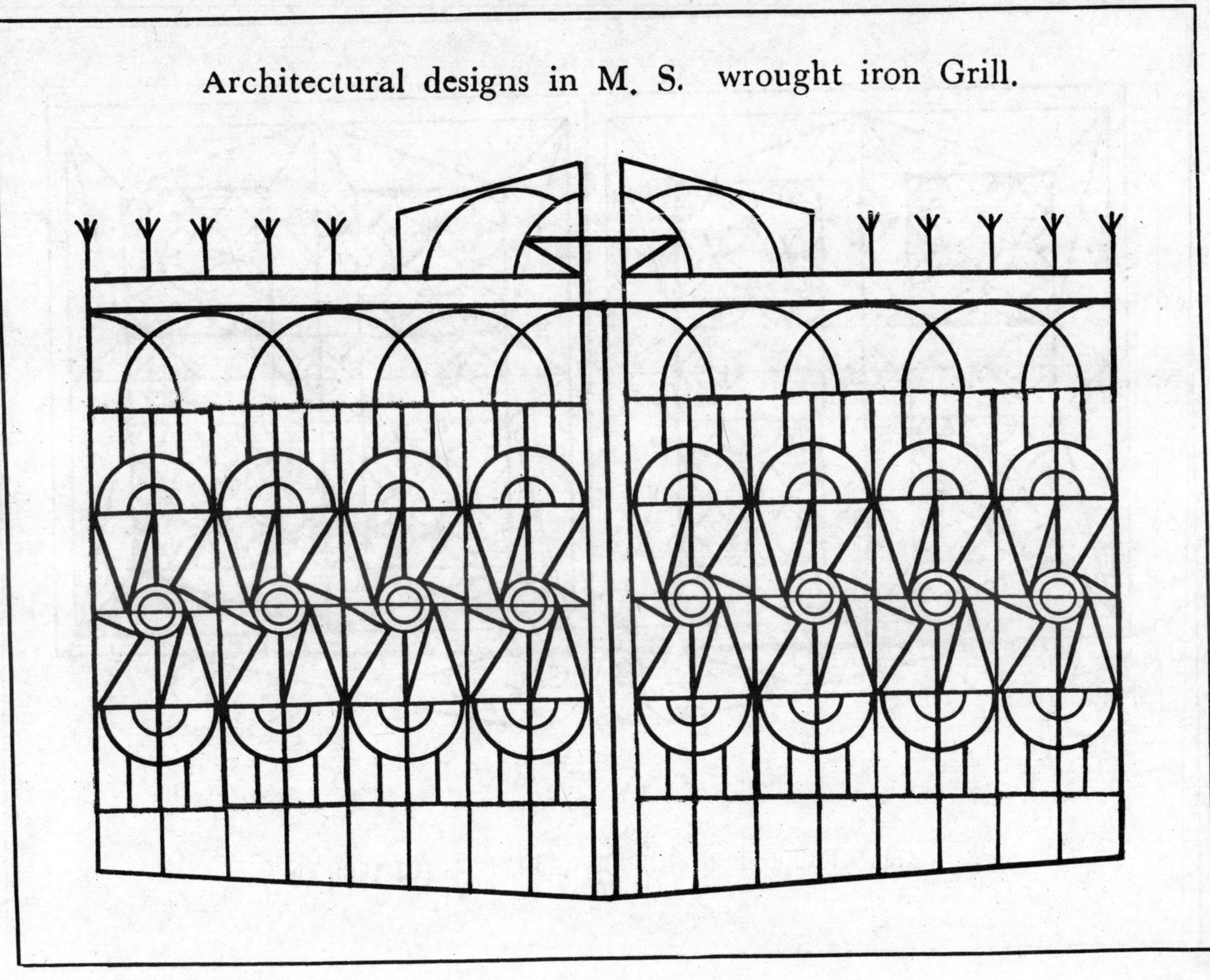

A beatiful Flowery design of modern Art.

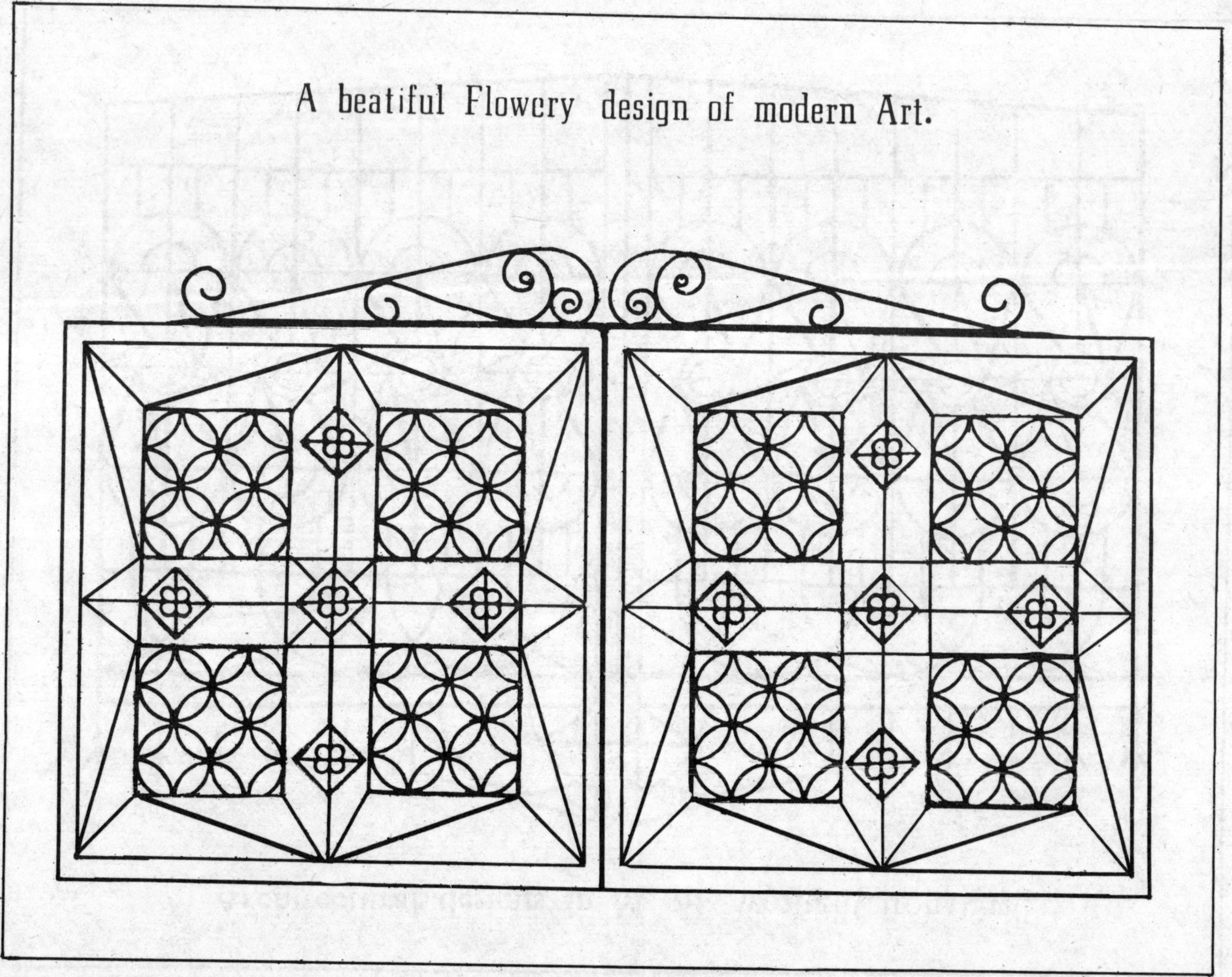

Charming design of leaves and rings for modernity.

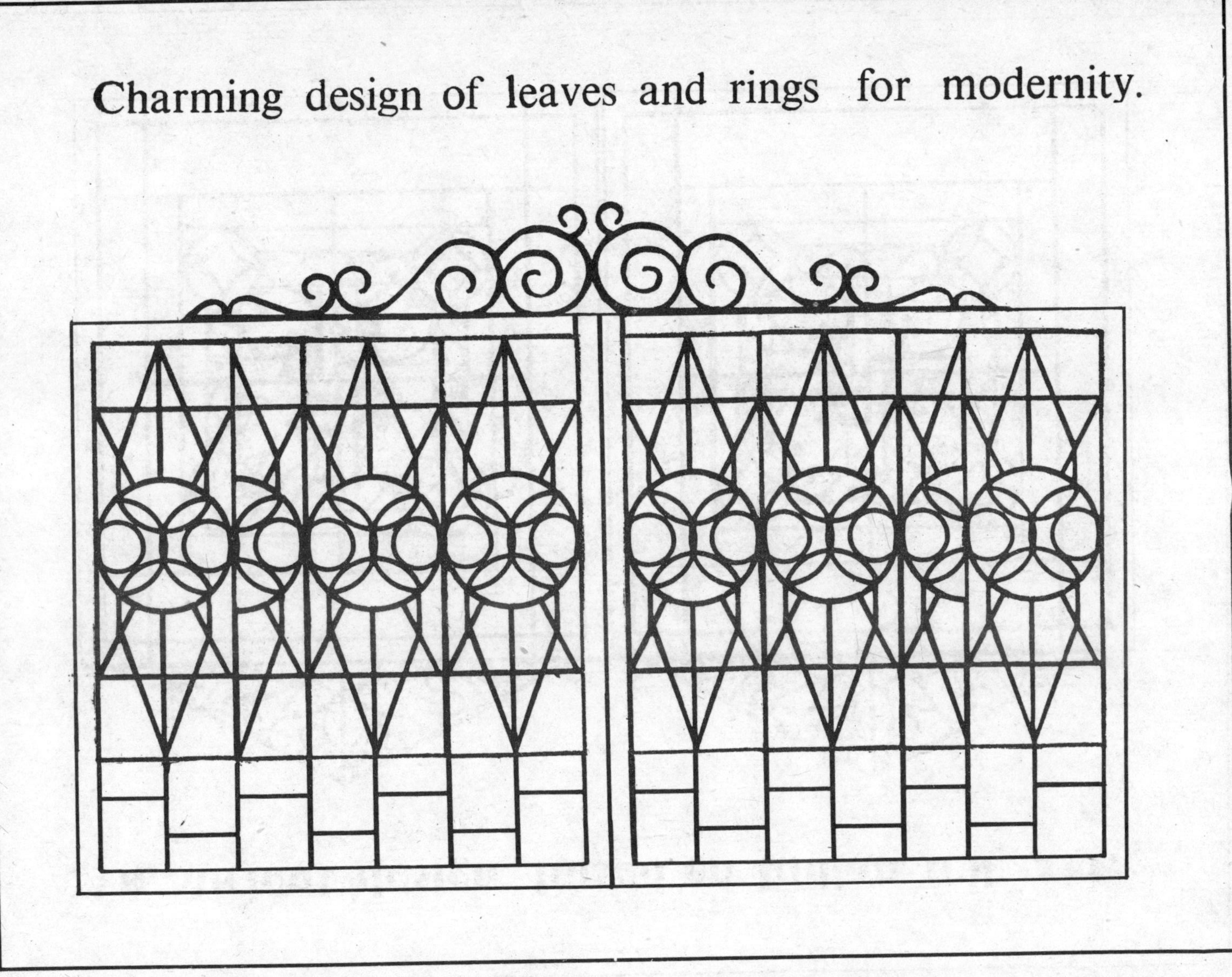

An ancient design based on Indian folk Art.

Very beautiful designs of modern decoration.

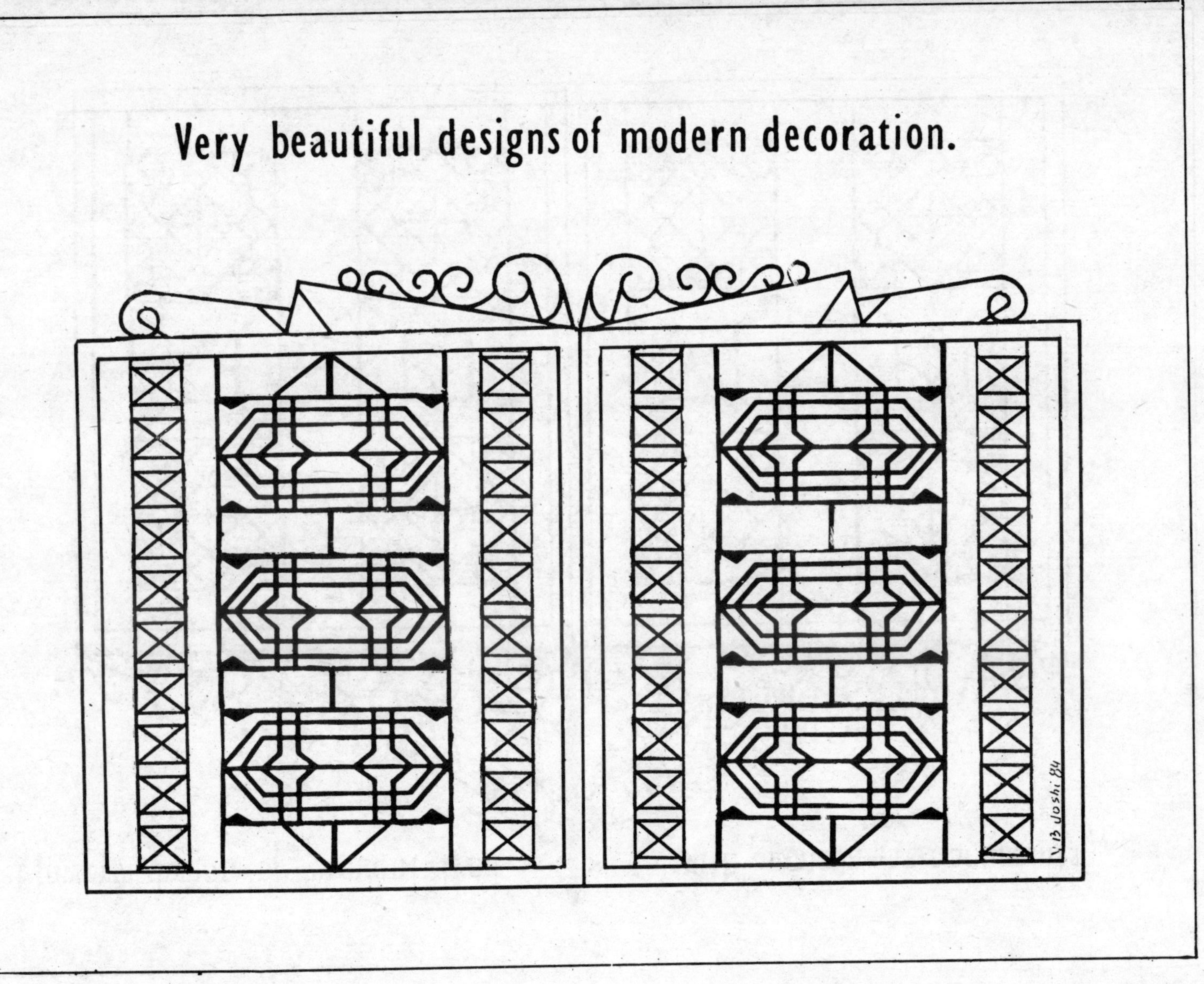

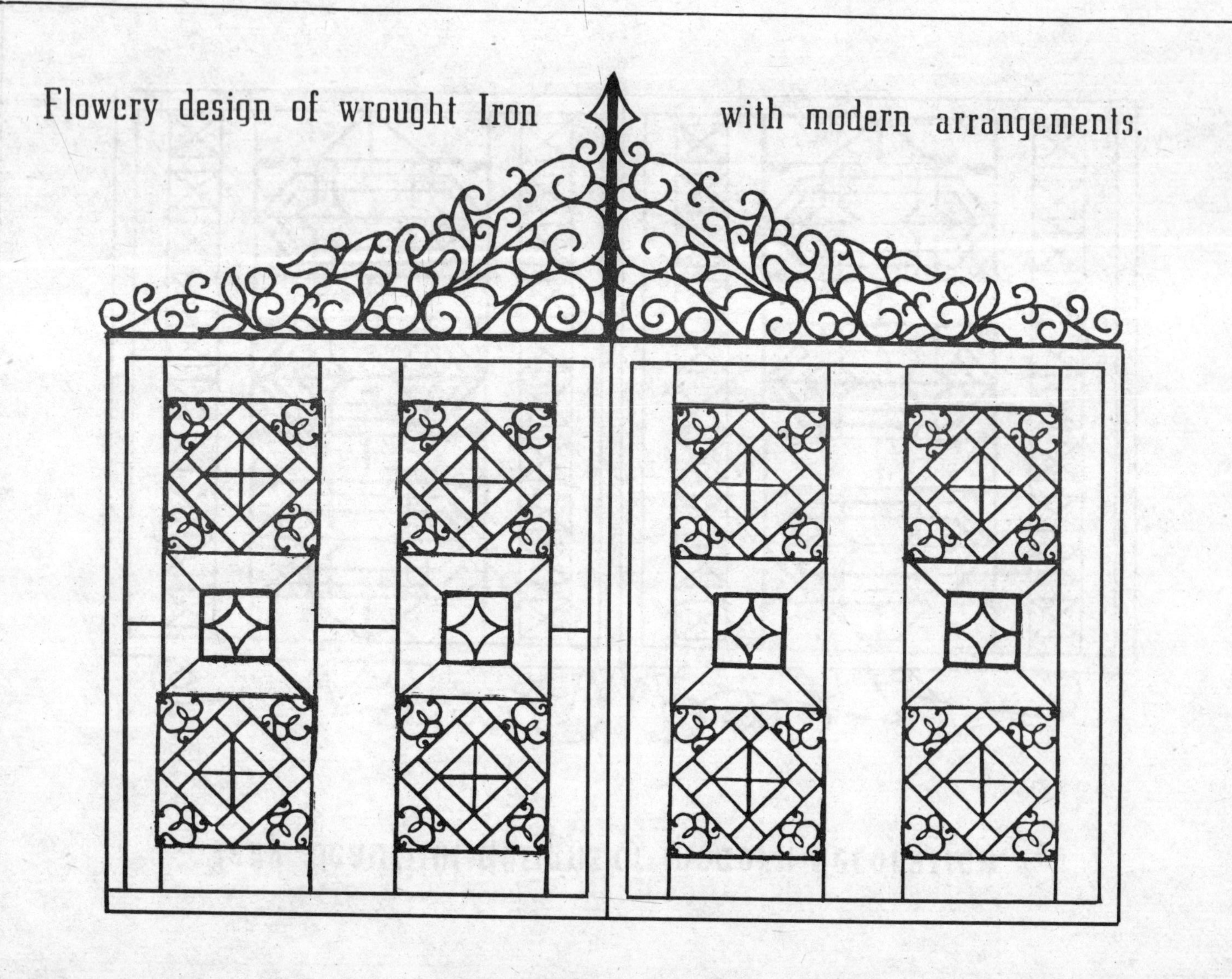

Flowery design of wrought Iron with modern arrangements.

Ultra-modern design of circular steel sheet, very-famous in West-Germany.

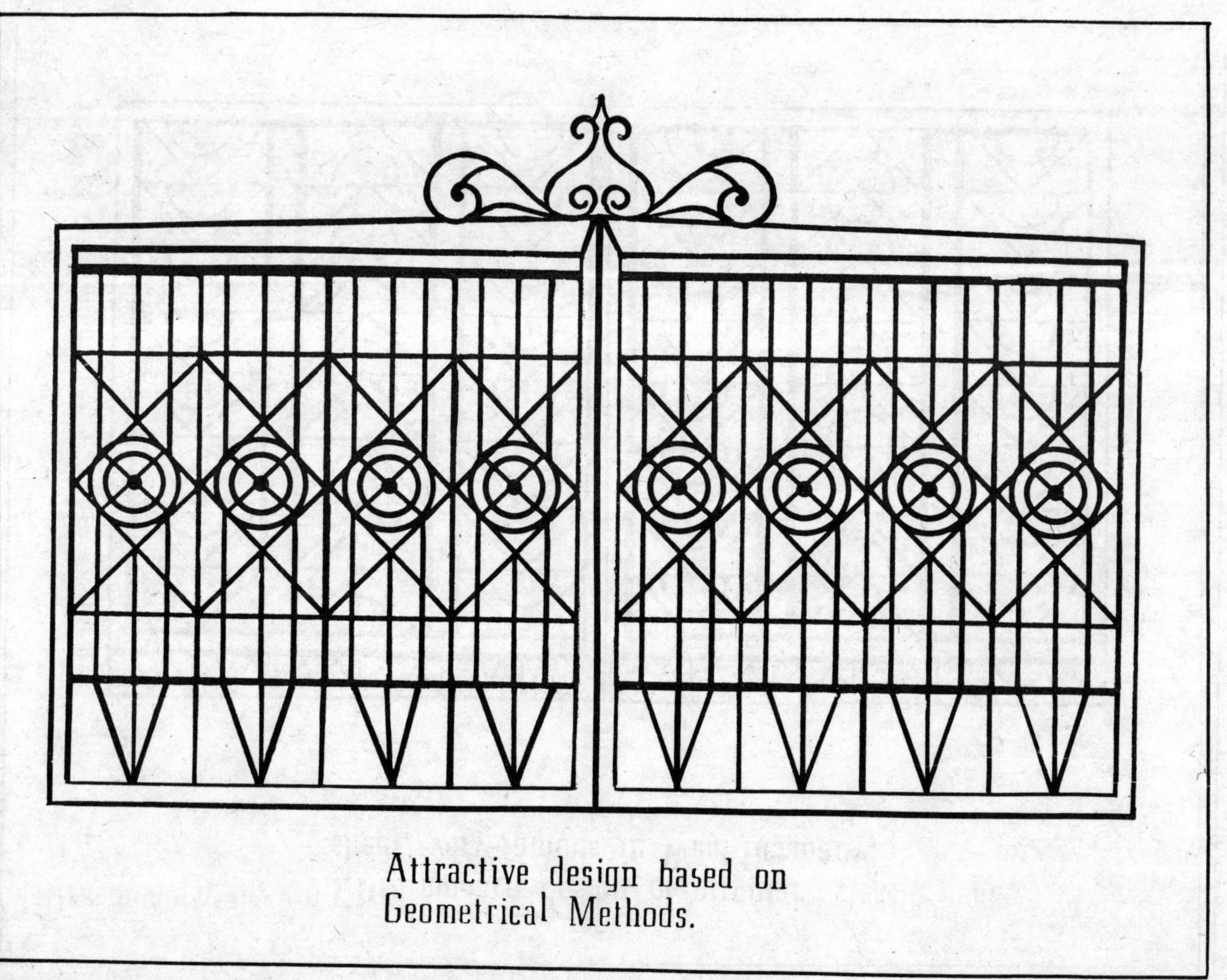

Attractive design based on Geometrical Methods.

Ultra-modern design of modern Art.

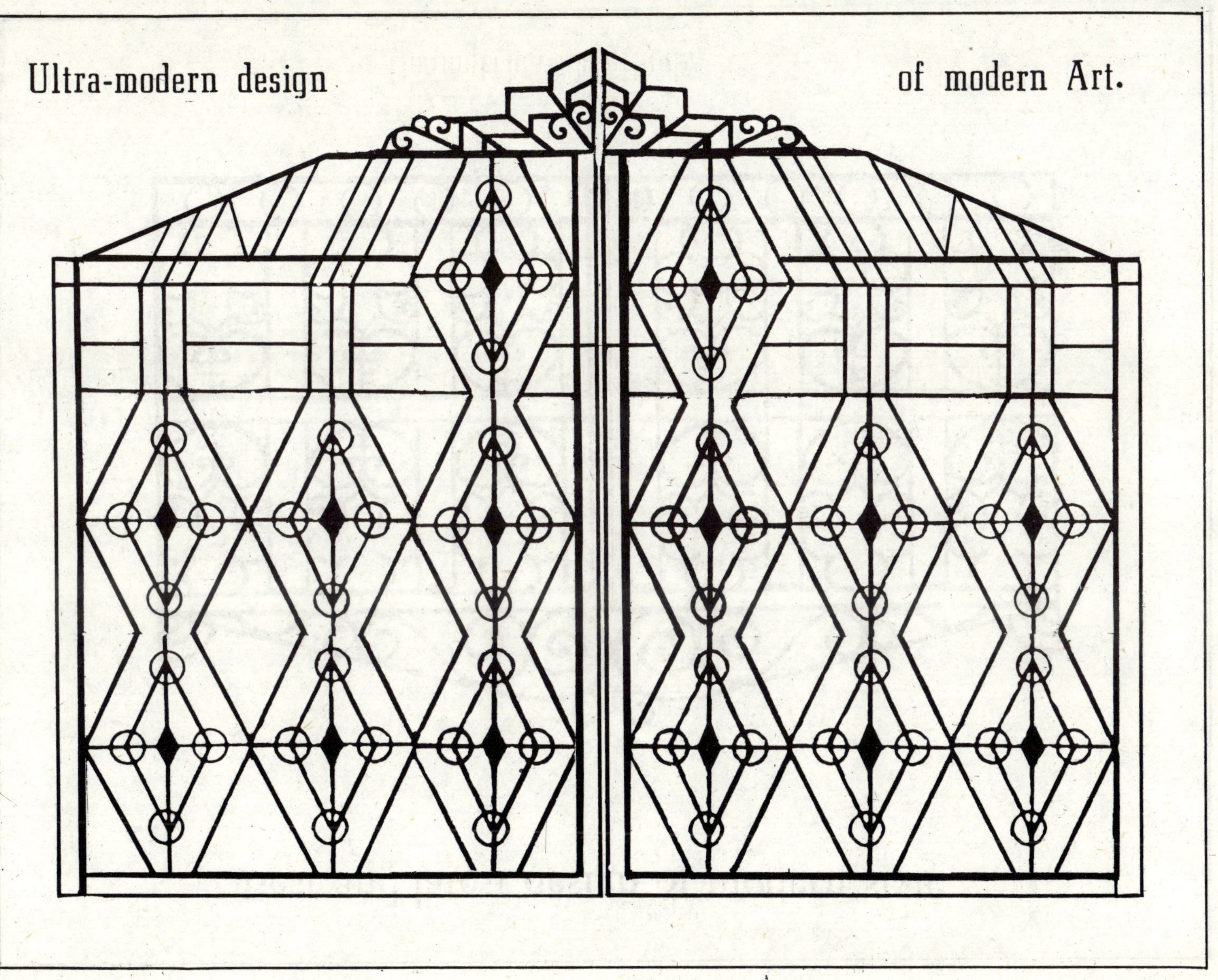

Best and latest design of modern style

Ancient design of Gates for Garden and Railway Gates

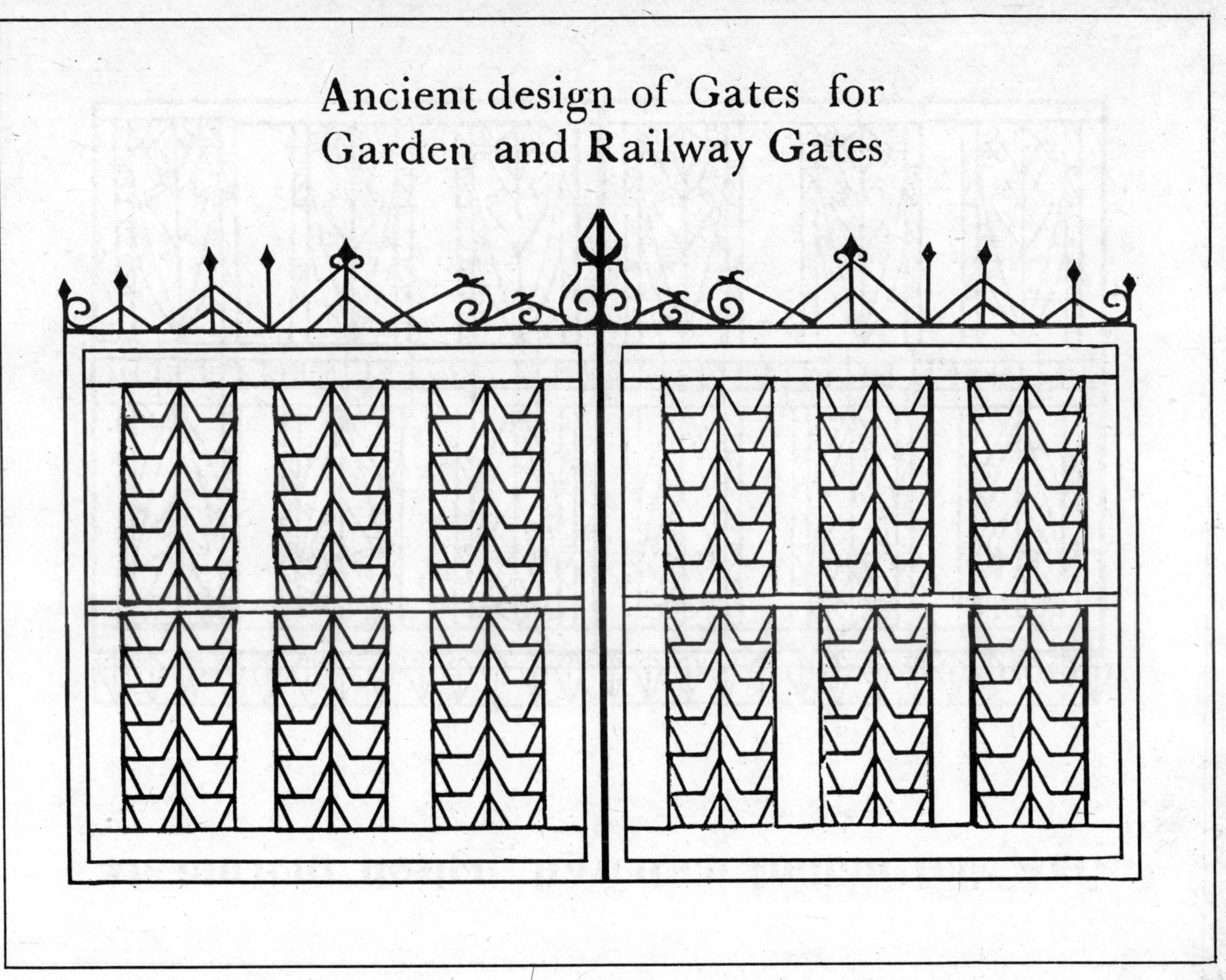

An ancient design based on Indian folk Art.

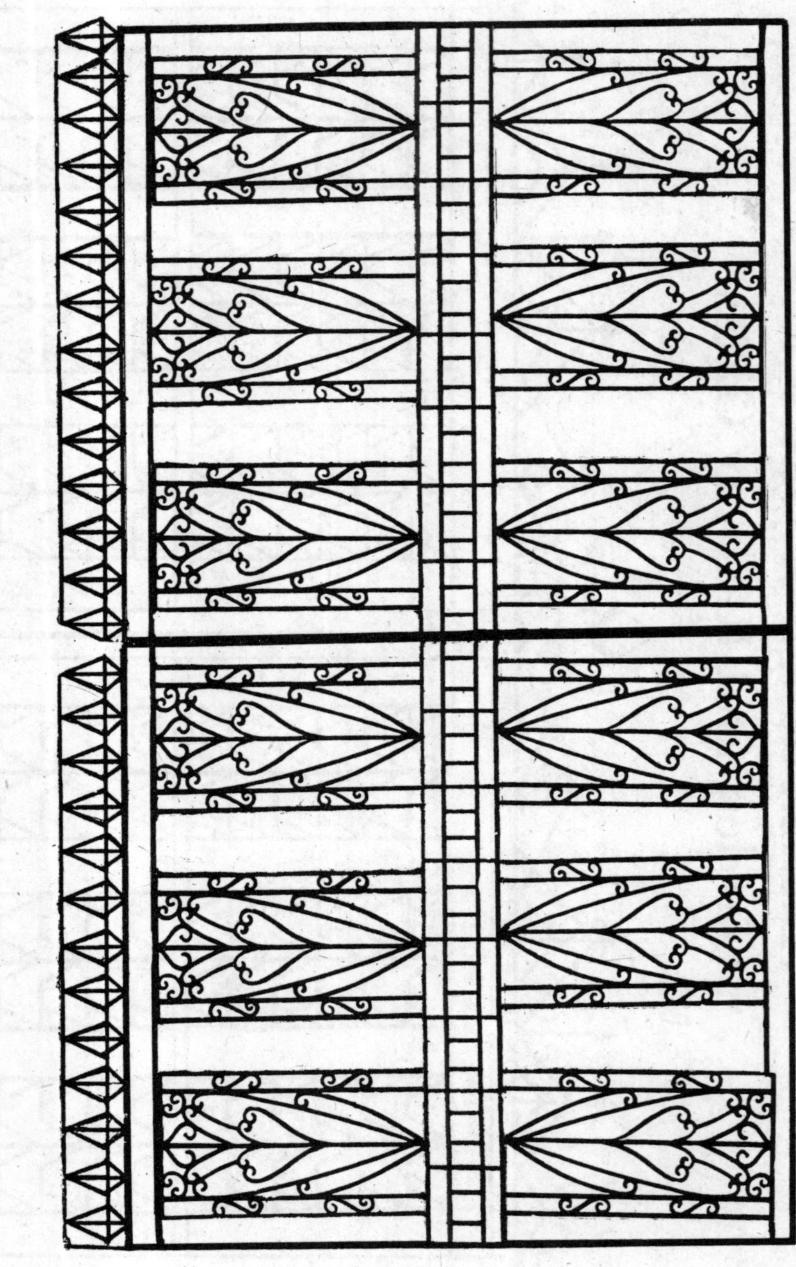

Good all purpose designs of Grills.

A Common design of Gate for decoration of well Planned Building.

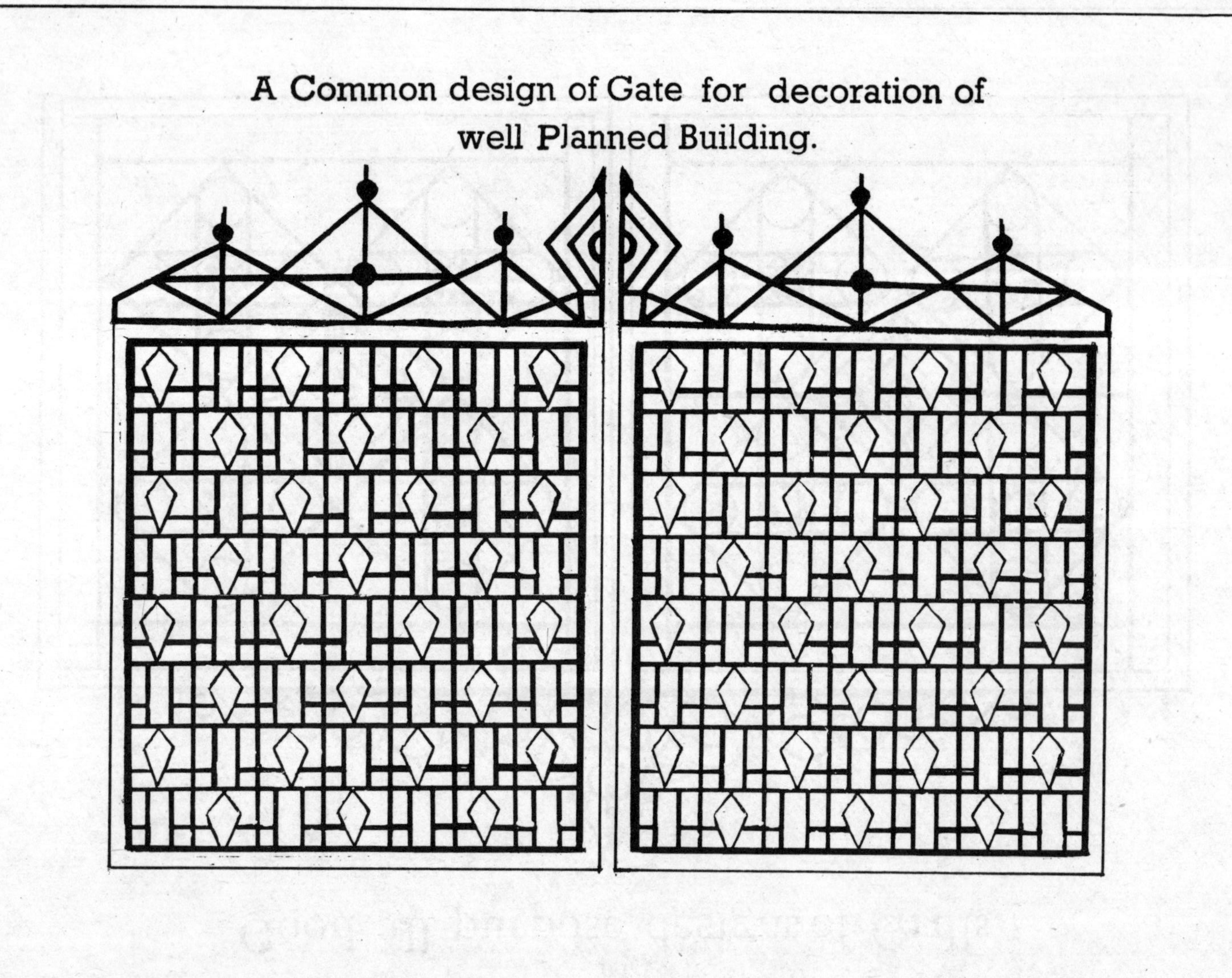

Charming design of leaves and rings for modernity.

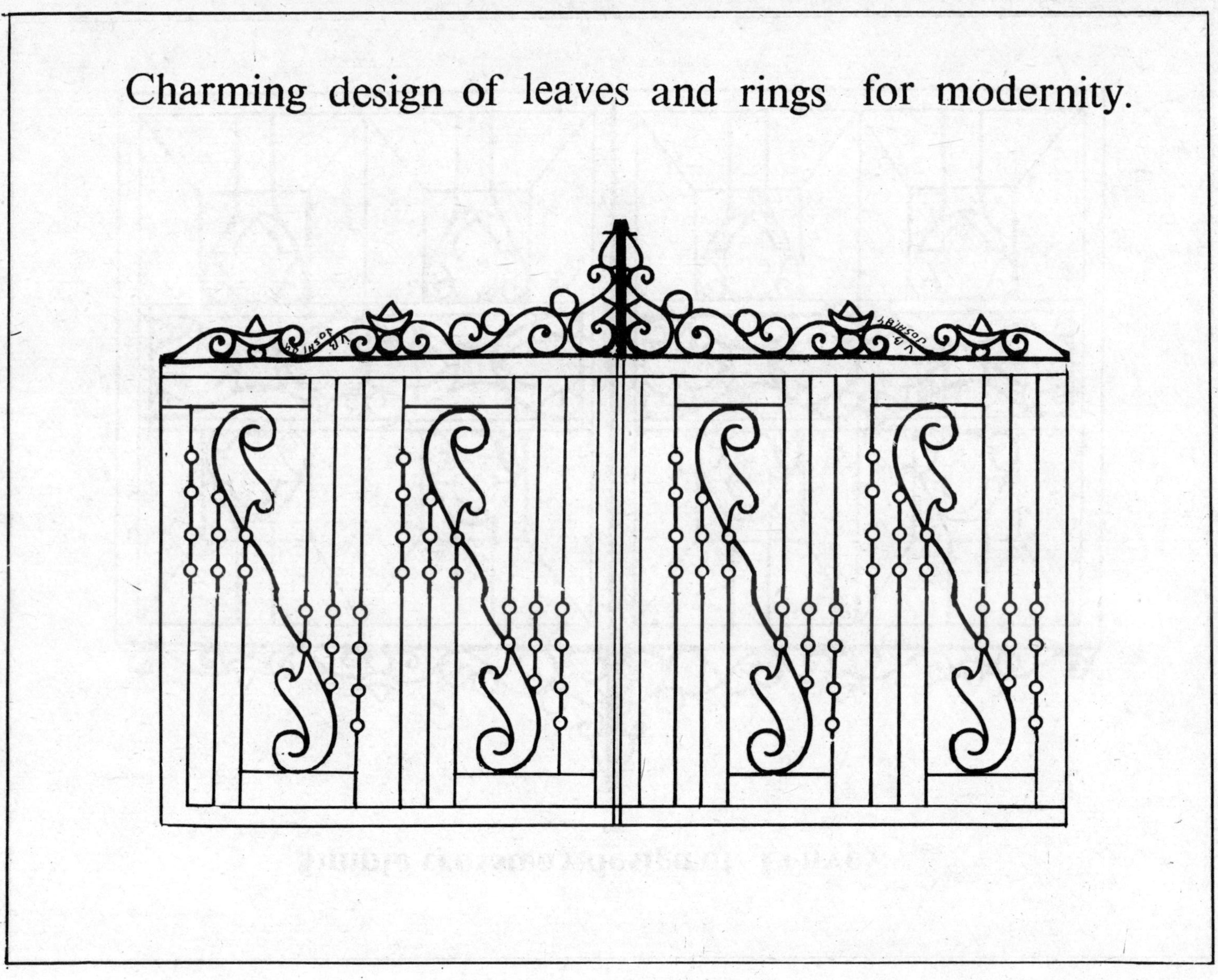

Simple crossway design of Leaves.

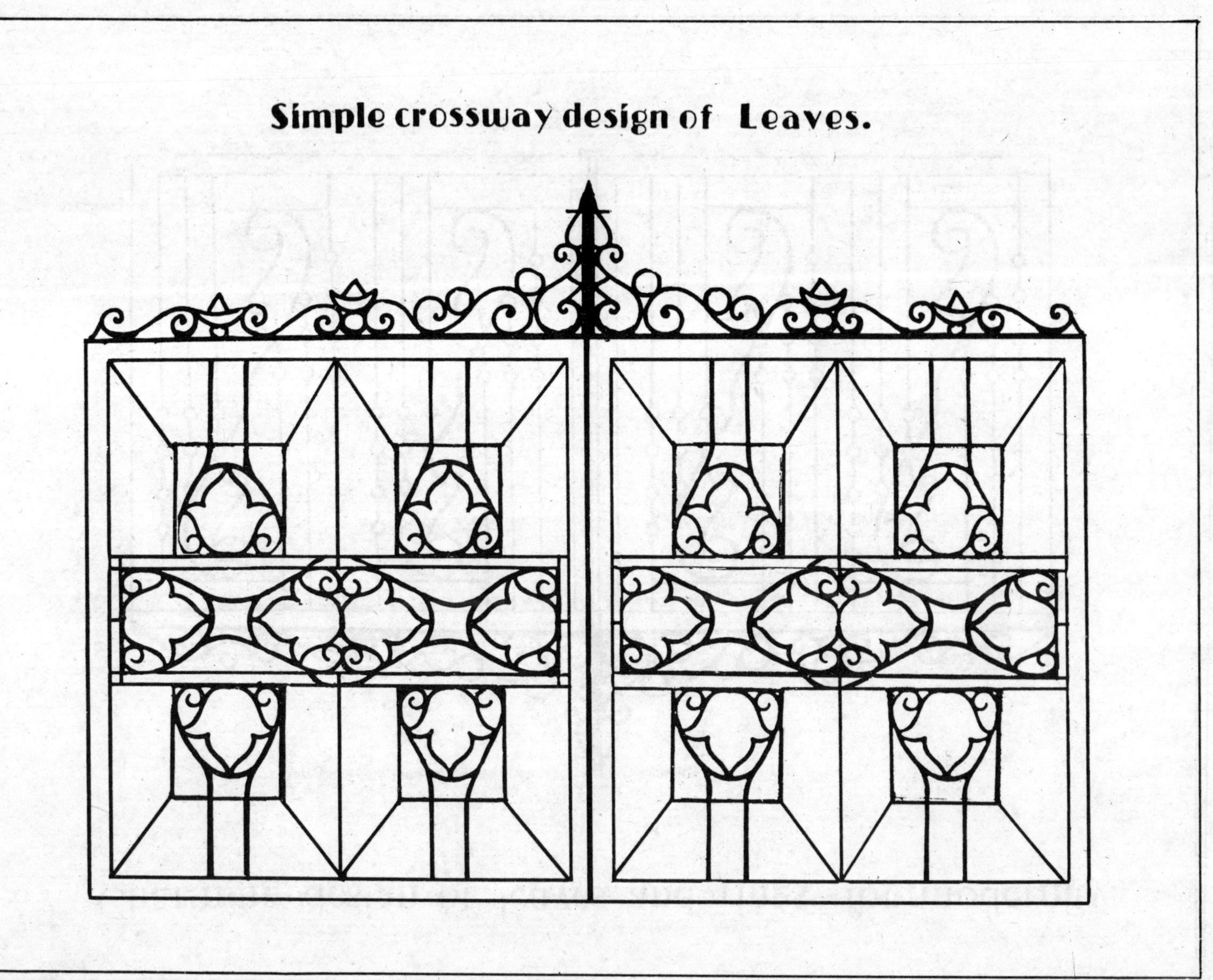

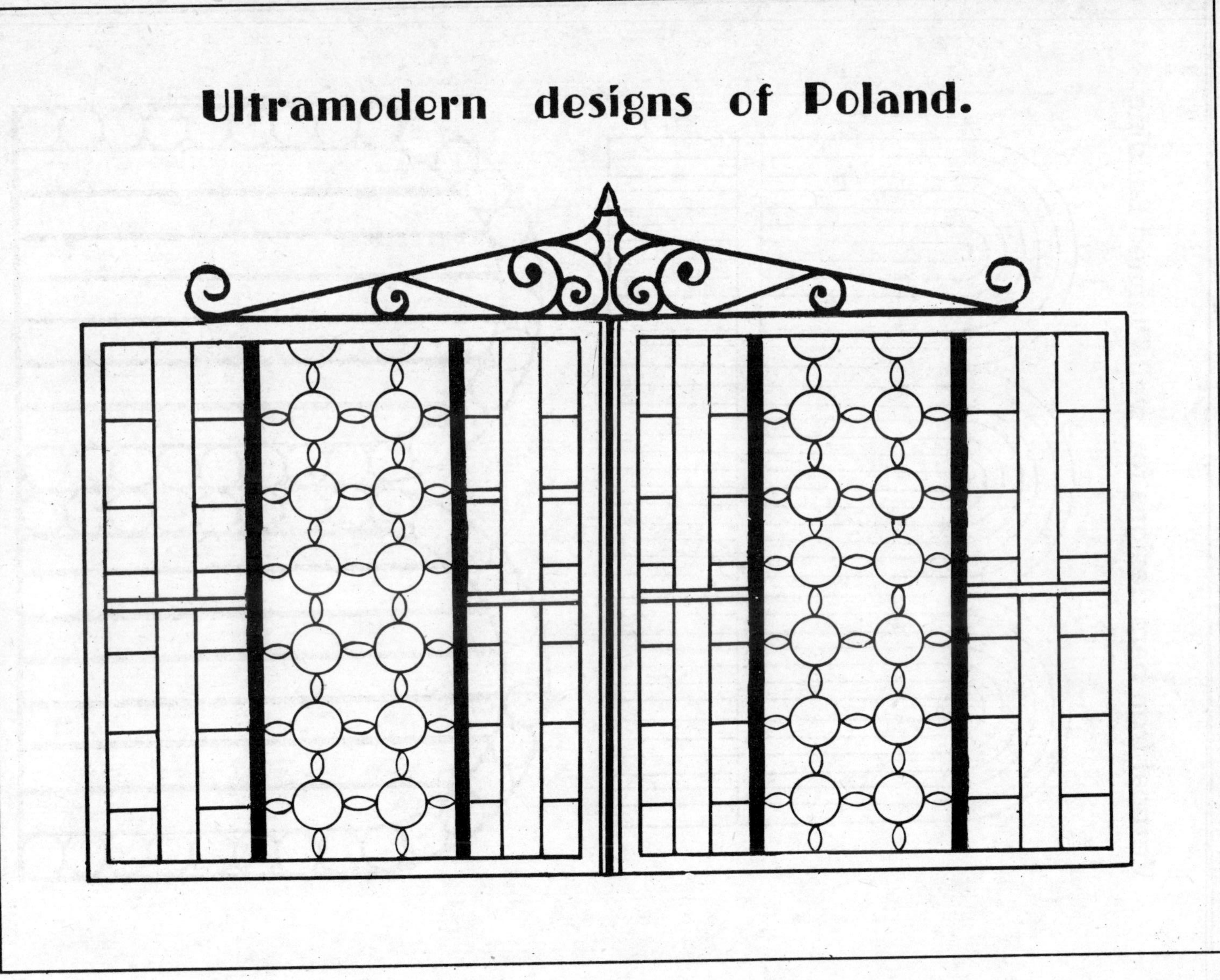

Ultramodern designs of Poland.

Vertical Iron bars designs for well Planned Building.

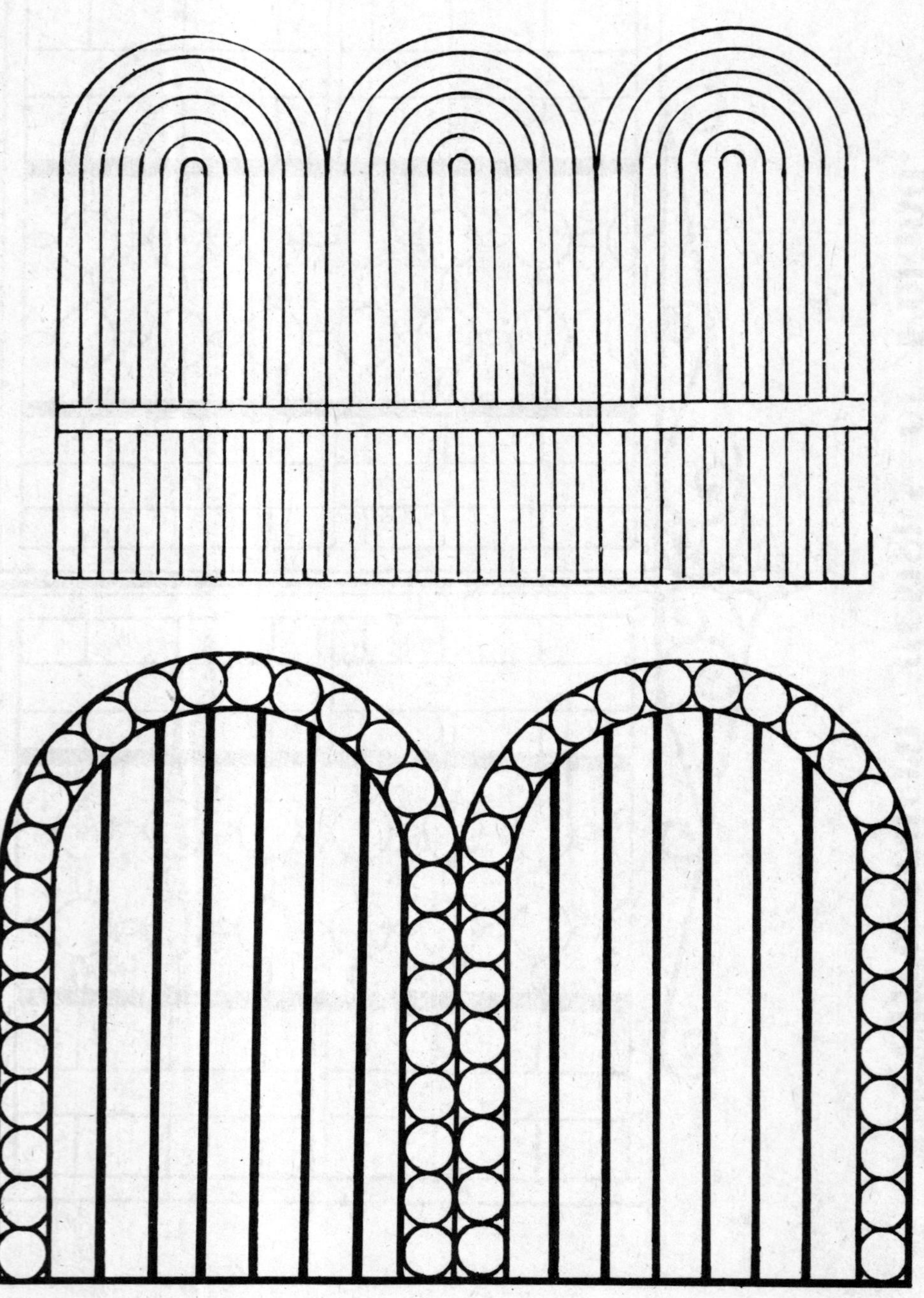

Straight Iron bar designs with symitrical arrangement.

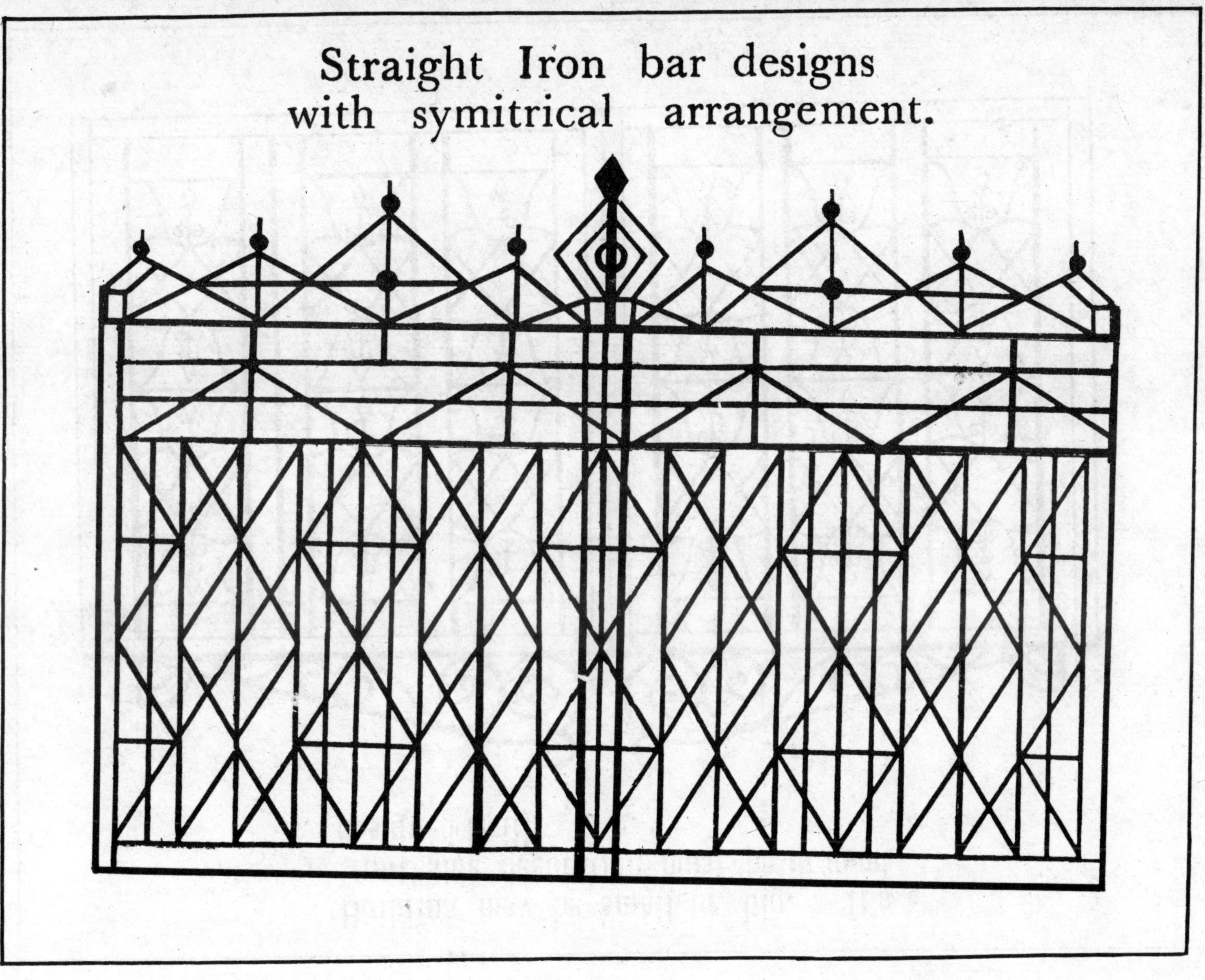

Building mav be small or big. It's front side decoration must be of good designed Grills.

A composition of modern design of net adjustment.

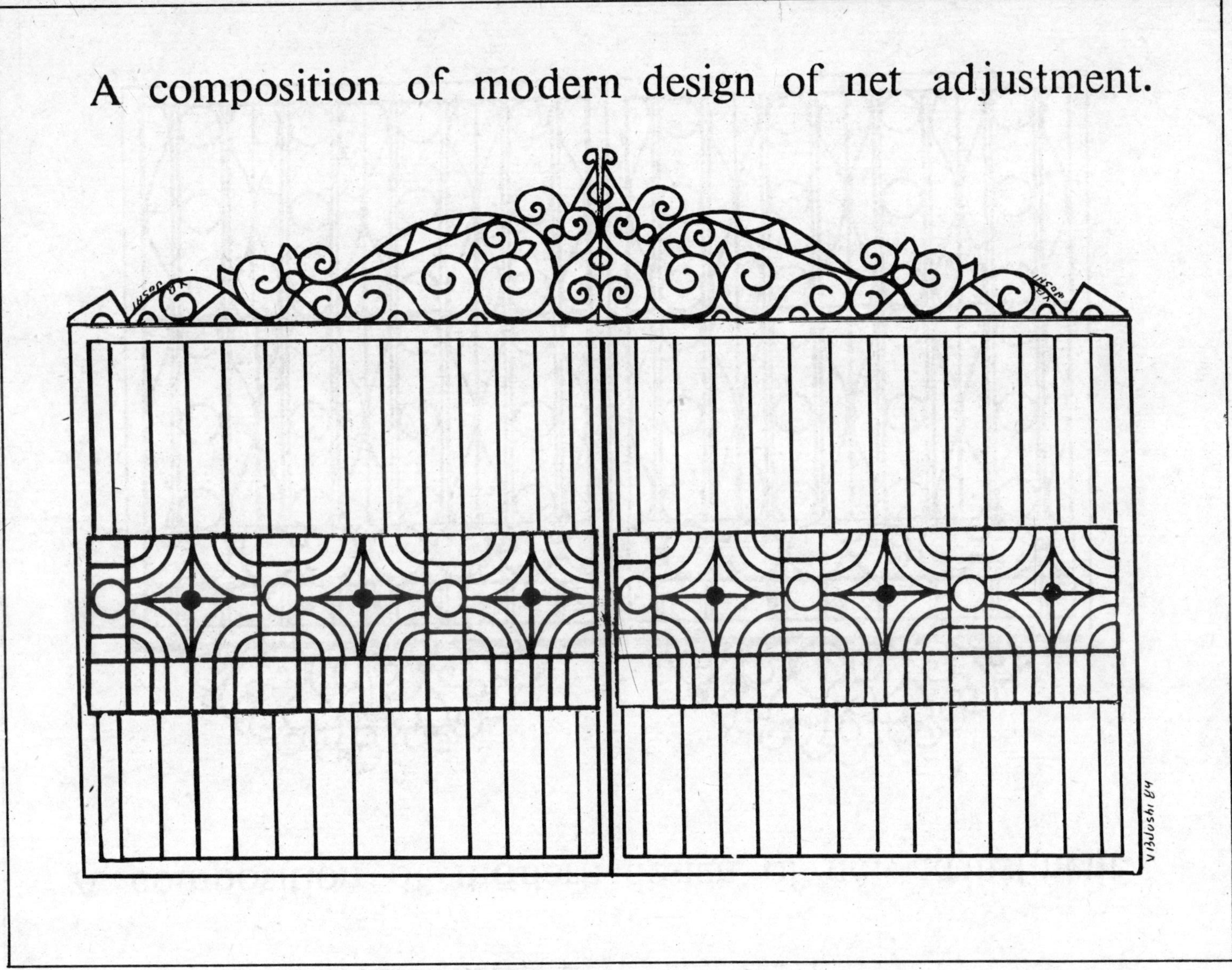

A composition of modern design of new adjustment.

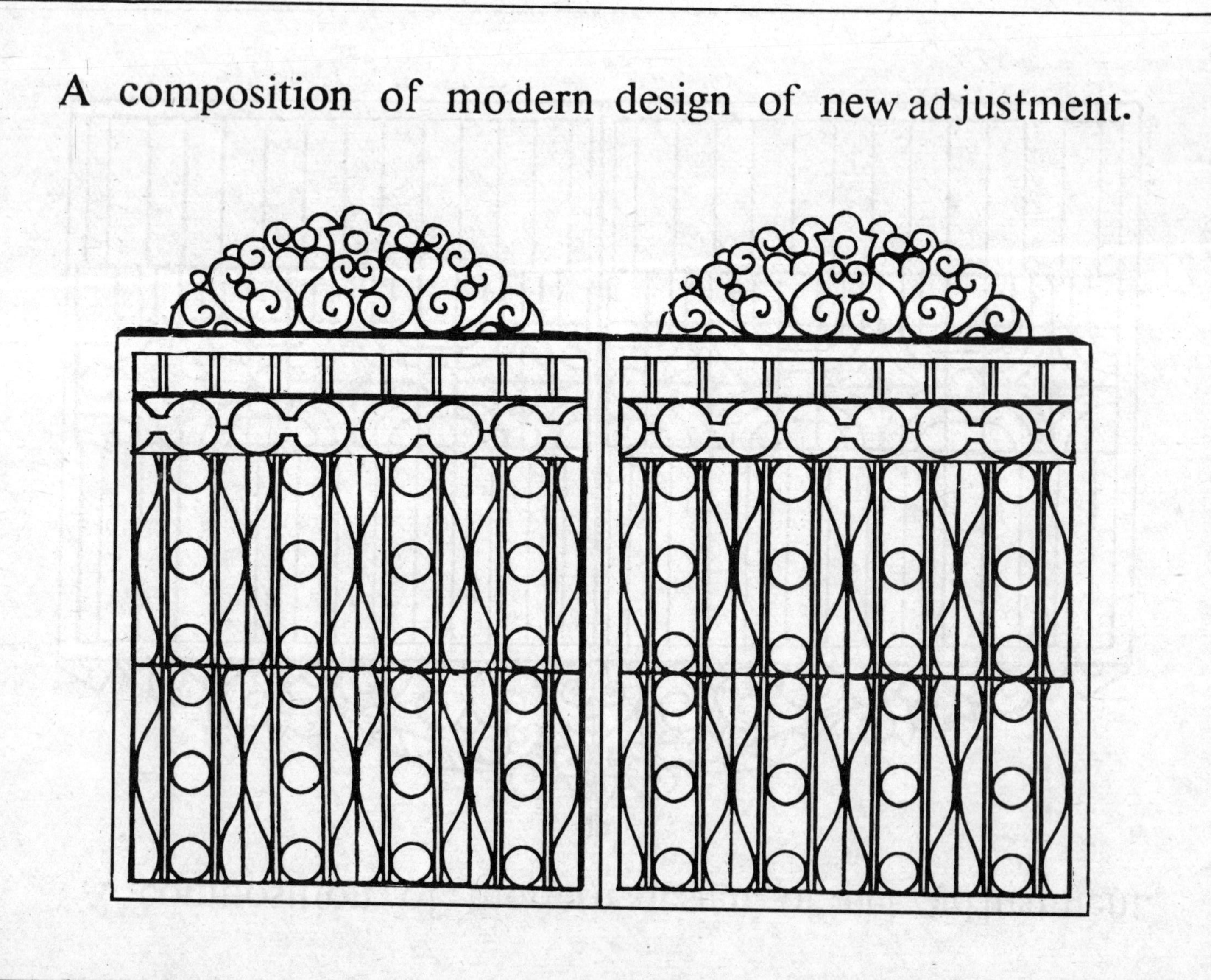

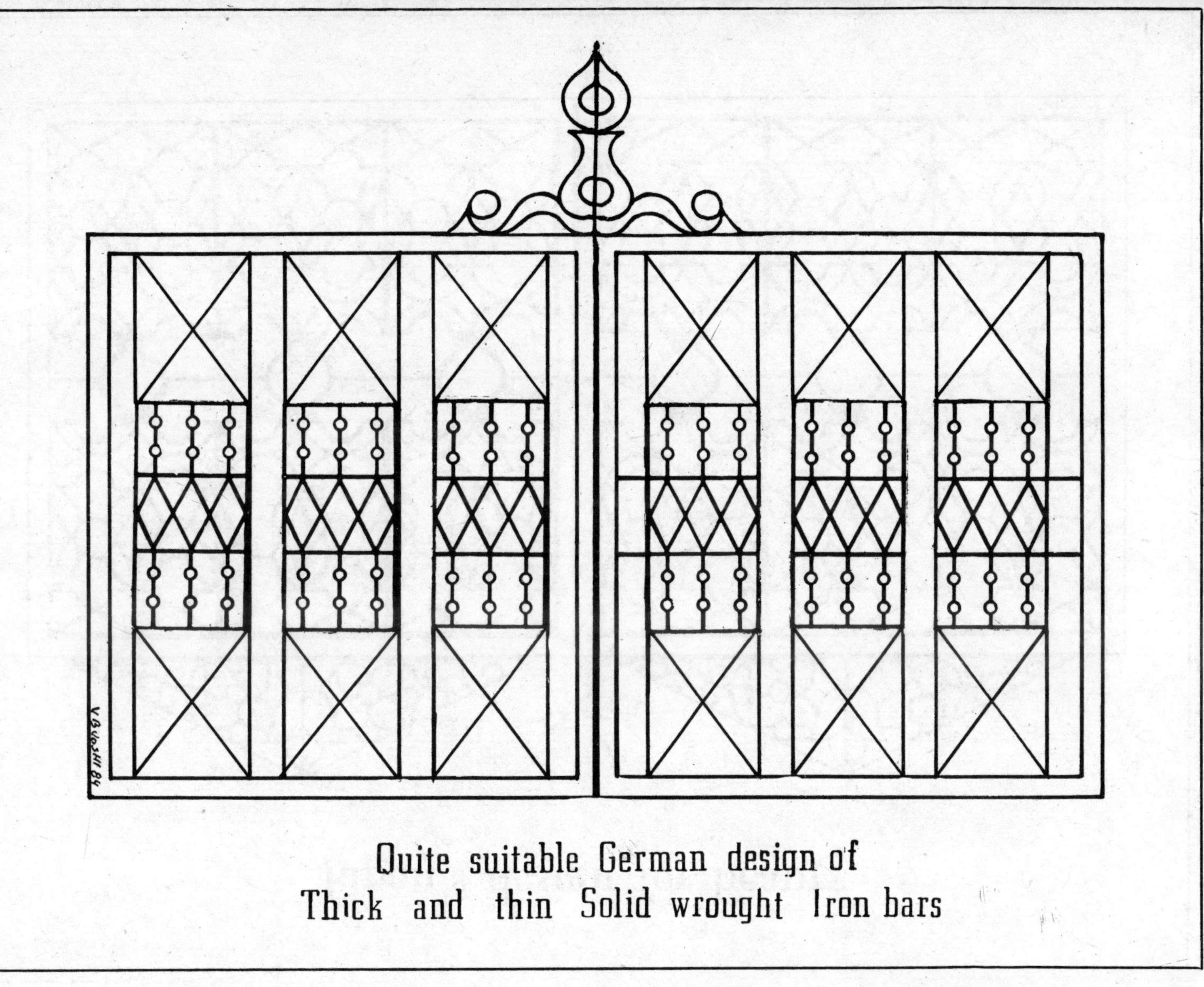

Quite suitable German design of
Thick and thin Solid wrought Iron bars

Japan's design for beauty

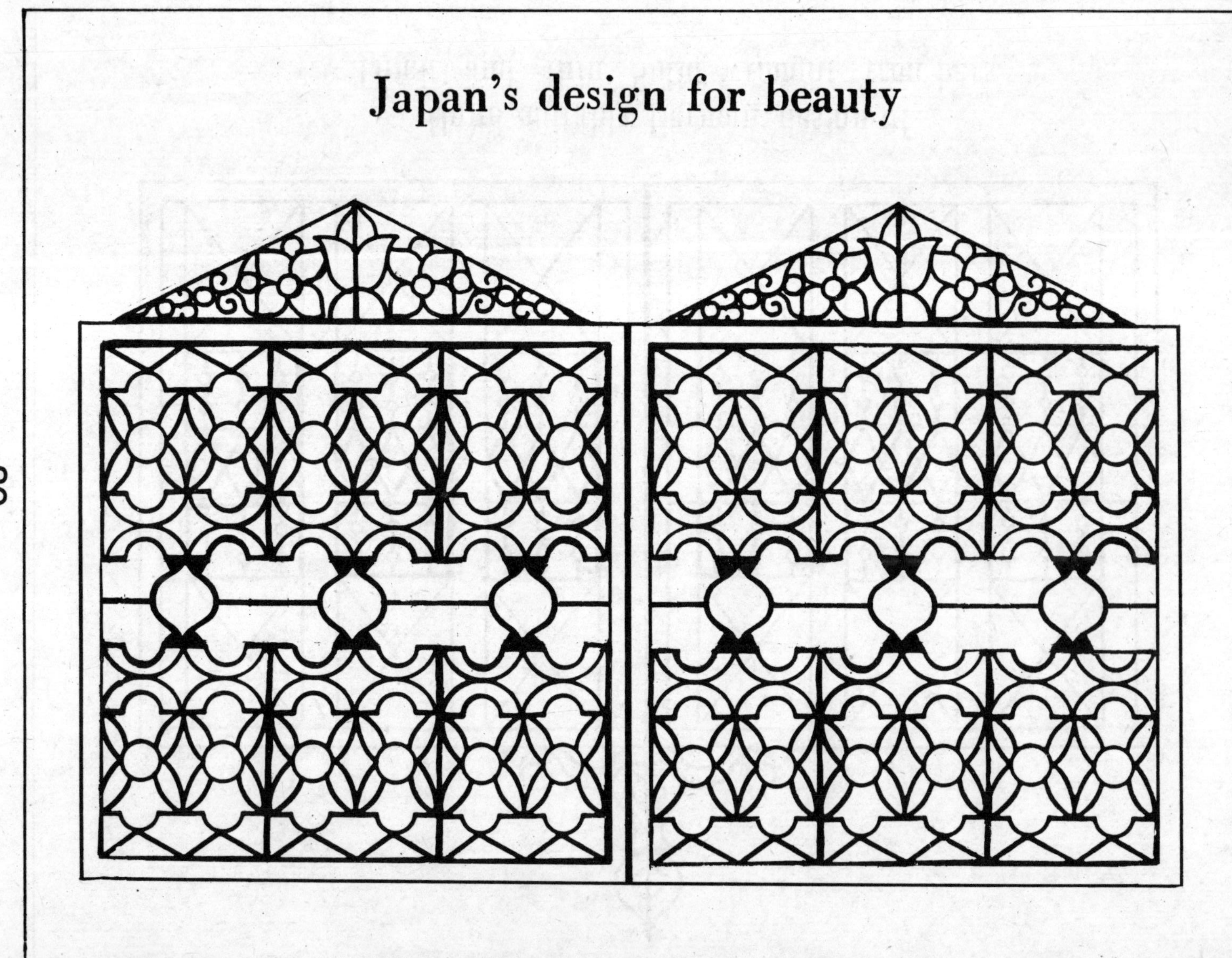

CATALOGUE 2014

PUSTAK MAHAL®

J-3/16, Daryaganj, New Delhi-110002
Ph.: 23276539, 23272783-84, Fax: 011-23260518

FREE Tutorial CD

Big Size 18.5 x 24 cm
Pages over 392 0004 R

FREE Tutorial CD

Big Size 18.5 x 24 cm
Pages 368 0008 R

FREE Tutorial CD

Big Size 18.5 x 24 cm
Pages over 368 0007 R

FREE Tutorial DVD

Big Size 18.5 x 24 cm
Pages 384 0001 R

With a CD for learning correct pronounciation of English and other language

A 14-Volume series teaching 6 Regional Languages through Hindi & vice versa

1232 A - Assamese-Hindi	1221 S - Tamil-Hindi
1233 B - Hindi-Assamese	1223 S - Telugu-Hindi
1215 S - Hindi-Tamil	1224 S - Bangla-Hindi
1217 S - Hindi-Telugu	1225 S - Gujarati-Hindi
1218 S - Hindi-Bangla	1222 S - Kannada-Hindi
1219 S - Hindi-Gujarati	1128 B - Hindi-Arabic
1216 S - Hindi Kannada	1220 S - Malayalam-Hindi
1236 A - Malayalam-Arabic	1214 S - Hindi-Malayalam

FREE Tutorial DVD

12 S Big Size 18.5 x 24 cm
Pages 368

FREE Tutorial DVD

Big Size 18.5 x 24 cm
Pages 384 0002 R

Big Size 18.5 x 24 cm
Pages 264 9694 J

FREE Tutorial CD

Big Size 18.5 x 24 cm
Pages 352 1234 S

Pages 252-256 in each

6611 G - English – Hindi
1133 A - English – Bangla
1132 D - English – Tamil
1134 B - English – Kannada
1136 D - English – Telugu
1137 A - English – Gujarati
1135 C - English – Malayalam

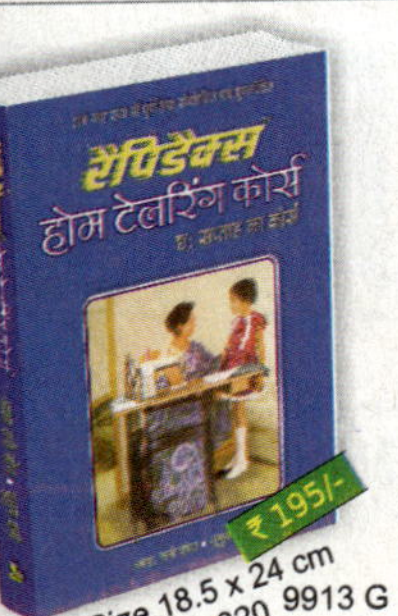

Big Size 18.5 x 24 cm
Pages 320 9913 G

9742 C Size 13.5 x 19.5 cm
Pages 464

0003 R Size 14 x 21.5 cm
Pages 584

9661 M Size 13.5 x 19.5 cm
Pages 576

6607 L

...lish-Hindi, English-Tamil, English-Kannada
...lish-Telugu, English-Urdu, English-Assamese
...lish-Bangla, English-Odia, English-Malayalam
...lish-Marathi, English-Gujarati

PICTURE DICTIONARY — All in Colour

100/- each

Over 1200 entries with coloured pictures

English-Hindi, English- Marathi
English-Odia, English-Kannada
English-Tamil, English-Telugu
English-Nepali, English-Assamese
English-Bangla

अंग्रेजी के 10000 से अधिक शब्द
हर शब्द के अनेक अर्थ
अर्थानुसार प्रयोग

Compact Edition — Rapidex English-Hindi Compact Dictionary

₹ 62/- each

Compact Size 10.2x12.7 cm
Pages 384 in each

English-Hindi, English-Marathi,
English-Odia, English-Kannada,
English-Tamil, English-Telugu,
English-Nepali, English-Bangla
English to Punjabi & Hindi,
English-Assamese

Rapidex English-Hindi Dictionary with usages

₹ 155/- each

Size 13.5x19.5 cm
Pages 576 in each

Buy online at our website or at Leading Bookshops from:

PUSTAK MAHAL®
Delhi · Mumbai · Patna · Bengaluru
J-3/16, Daryaganj (Opposite Happy School), New Delhi -110002
Fax: 23260518 *email:* info@pustakmahal.com *Website:* www.pustakmahal.com

Buy from online Shopping Portals paying CASH ON DELIVERY at your doorstep
flipkart · HomeShop18 · snapdeal · amazon.in · uRead.com

Authors/Writers are invited to submit their manuscripts through our website.

POPULAR SCIENCE

9496 A • Rs. 120/-

2215 S • ₹ 150/- Available in Hindi also.

Contains: 10 Projects

2214 S • ₹ 150/- Available in Hindi also.

FREE Tutorial CD

Set Code: 4514 S

- Over 900 Illustrati
- Over 800 Pages
- 890 Articles
- Four Volumes

FREE Buy all 4 Vols. & get 5th Volume free with an Audio-Video DVD worth ₹ 135/-

Set 4 Vols.: ₹ 780
Each Vol.: ₹ 195

Available in Hindi & English both

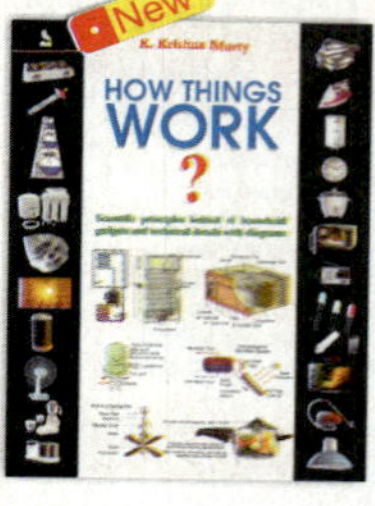

8702 B• ₹ 150/-

HC009 • ₹ 620/-

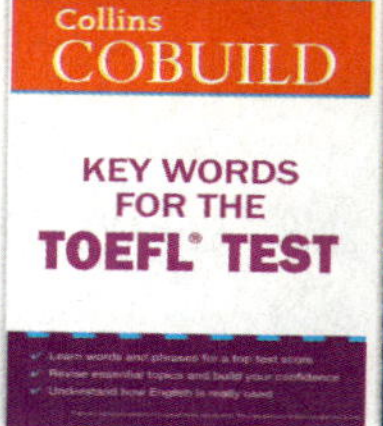

HC008 • ₹ 399/-

HC005 • ₹ 540/-

This Library is must for every student of a School or a College

Also equally useful for everyone else

Price: ₹ 600/-

Contains 4 books of ₹ 150/- each

9412 C • ₹ 120/-

6678 D • ₹ 195/-

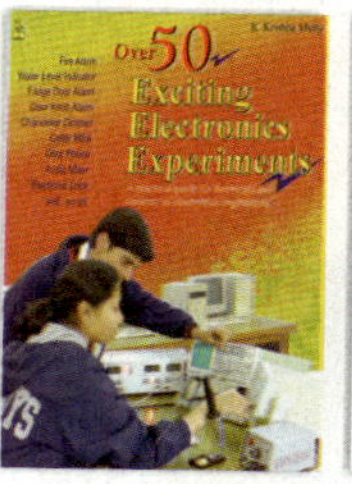

6679 A • ₹ 150/-

9660 K • ₹ 250/-

4 Books of the Library

₹ 150/- Page 256 (with CD) English Conversation

₹ 150/- Page 310 Grammar & Punctuation

₹ 150/- Page 316 How to use English

₹ 150/- Page 344 English Vocabu

QUIZ BOOKS

8965 D • ₹ 150/-

7726 K • ₹ 100/-

7727 L • ₹ 100/-

7723 F • ₹ 100/-

7722 E • ₹ 100/-

7753 G • ₹ 100/-

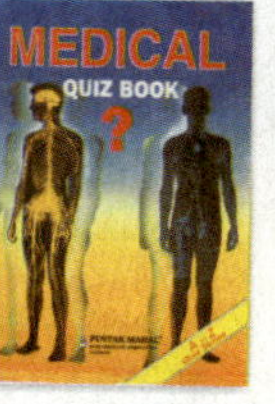

7725 B • ₹ 100/-

GENERAL BOOKS

9532 D • ₹ 250/- HB

8526 B • ₹ 125/-

8712 M • ₹ 150/-

8711 K • ₹ 19

9821 K • ₹ 175/-

9699 T • ₹ 100/-

9767 B • ₹ 150/-

5114 B • ₹ 88

4175 A • ₹ 195/-

9459 H • ₹ 1000/- (HB)

9041 A • ₹ 195/-

4022 D • ₹ 10

SELF-IMPROVEMENT

New

R • ₹ 195/- 9498 C • ₹ 180/- 9490 H • ₹ 175/- 9464 R • ₹ 80/- 9096 B • ₹ 120/- 5614 E • ₹ 150/- 4008 J • ₹ 120/- 9026 D • ₹ 120/- 9786 M • ₹ 195/-

1 J • ₹ 100/- 8885 D • ₹ 80/- 9081 D • ₹ 150/- 9091 B • ₹ 120/- 9060 B • ₹ 120/- 9684 F • ₹ 195/- 8928 D • ₹ 80/- 9449 A • ₹ 195/- 9788 R • ₹ 195/-

MANAGEMENT/JOB/CARRIER/BUSINESS & PROFESSION

61 K • ₹ 135/- 5338 A • ₹ 135/- with CD 8979 A • ₹ 120/- 9406 B • ₹ 150/- 5441 D • ₹ 195/- 8883 D • ₹ 120/- 9672 G • ₹ 150/- 9682 D • ₹ 120/-

New

697 P • ₹ 195/- 9313 D • ₹ 150/- 5623 B • ₹ 195/- 9439 L • ₹ 150/- 4005 E • ₹ 150/- 5643 B • ₹ 120/- 9431 C • ₹ 175/- 8990 C • ₹ 96/-

018 D • ₹ 150/- 9079 B • ₹ 195/- 5618 D • ₹ 120/- 5640 C • ₹ 120/- 5615 D • ₹ 150/- 8972 C • ₹ 80/- 4001 A • ₹ 150/- 5646 A • ₹ 225/- 4017 D • ₹ 120/-

PERSONALITY DEVELOPMENT

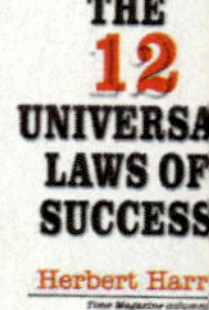

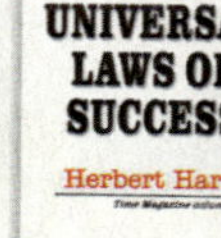

9670 E • ₹ 240/- 9678 R • ₹ 195/- 9450 B • ₹ 195/- 9487 E • ₹ 150/- 9466 T • ₹ 96/- 5639 B • ₹ 80/- 5641 A • ₹ 150/- 9088 C • ₹ 1

9667 B • ₹ 150/- 9666 A • ₹ 150/- 9696 M • ₹ 220/- 9973 B • ₹ 110/- 9981 B • ₹ 96/- 8868 D • ₹ 120/- 8966 E • ₹ 100/- 9070 B • ₹ 175/- 9028 D • ₹ 12

STUDENT DEVELOPMENT

9090 A • ₹ 195/- 9668 C • ₹ 150/- 9071 D • ₹ 140/- 9455 C • ₹ 150/- 5622 A • ₹ 108/- 9967 C • ₹ 120/- 2241 J • ₹ 100/- 94441 S • ₹ 195/-9654 D • ₹ 10

9652 D • ₹ 120/- 8962 A • ₹ 100/- 9089 D • ₹ 135/- 4016 D • ₹ 140/- 4009 K • ₹ 110/- 8997 B • ₹ 120/- 4010 L • ₹ 100/- 9787 P • ₹ 100/- 2244 D • ₹ 80/

SAYING/QUOTATIONS/PROVERBS

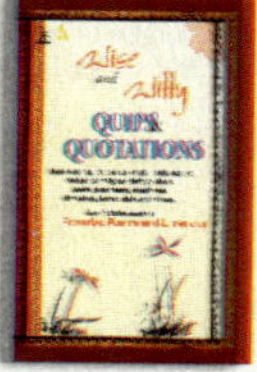

9474 F • ₹ 170/- 9789 A • ₹ 150/- 9953 A • ₹ 100/- 8947 E • ₹ 100/- 8999 D • ₹ 80/- 5512 A • ₹ 150/- 8963 B • ₹ 80/- 8890 D • ₹ 150/- 9925 A • ₹ 60/-

ALTERNATIVE THERAPIES

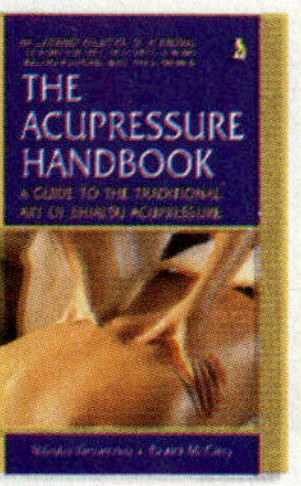

8882 F • ₹ 180/-

8983 E • ₹ 100/-

8836 D • ₹ 135/-

9935 F • ₹ 120/-

5637 D • ₹ 96/-

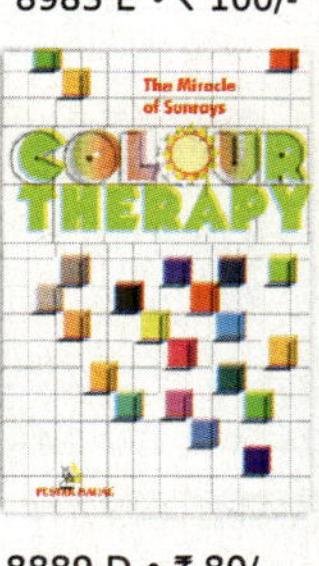

8889 D • ₹ 80/-

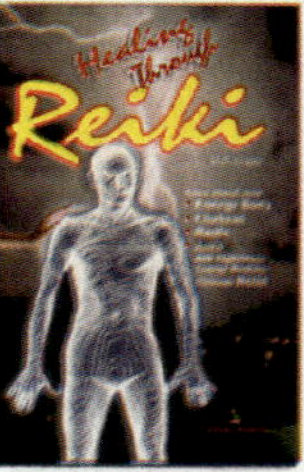

8842 D • ₹ 100/-

8941 A • ₹ 80/-

GENERAL HEALTH

9075 C • ₹ 225/-

8877 A • ₹ 120/-

9940 D • ₹ 150/-

8859 G • ₹ 80/-

9038 A • ₹ 68/-

8847 M • ₹ 100/- (H)

8870 D • ₹ 100/- (H)

9950 B • ₹ 120/-

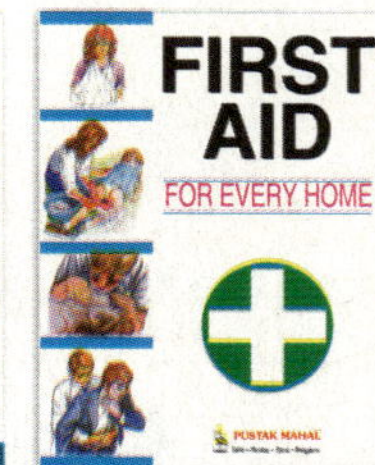

9902 F • ₹ 120/- (H)

COMMON AILMENTS & DISEASES

8891 D • ₹ 120/-

8281 A • ₹ 100/-

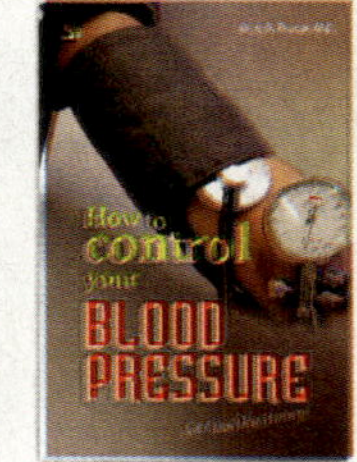

8094 D • ₹ 120/-

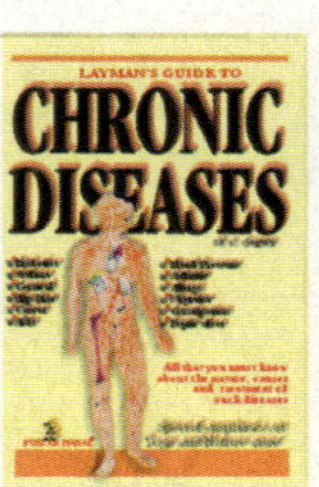

8848 D • ₹ 96/-

8276 A • ₹ 96/-

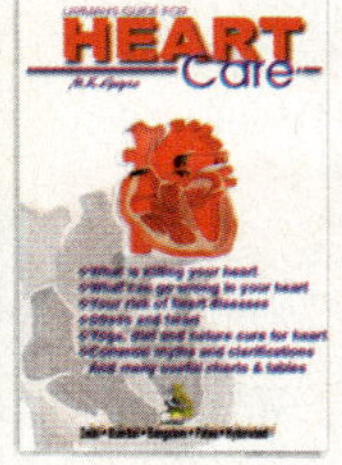

8888 D • ₹ 96/-

8908 D • ₹ 120/-

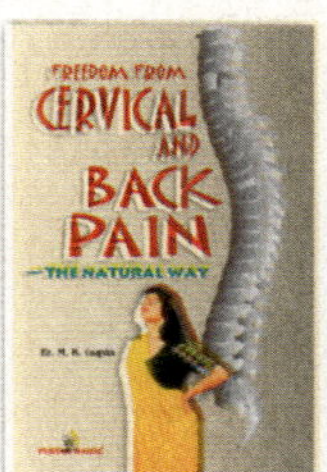

8878 B • ₹ 80/-

SLIMMING & FITNESS

8277 B • ₹ 120/-

8875 K • ₹ 120/-

9445 A • ₹ 150/-

DIET & NUTRITION

9941 D • ₹ 100/-

8904 D • ₹ 100/-

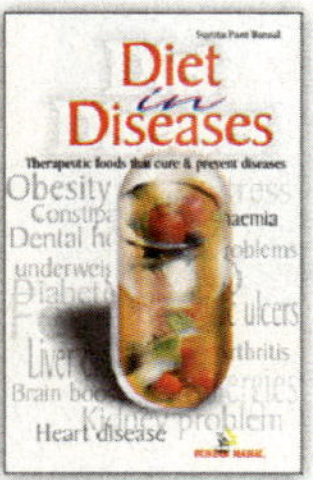

8985 B • ₹ 96/-

8968 G • ₹ 96/-

8271 C • ₹ 96/-

9037 D • ₹ 150/-

New

9873 C • ₹ 60/-

9770 E • ₹ 150/-

9799 D • ₹ 160/-

9453 A • ₹ 195/-

4179 A • ₹ 295/- (HB)

4128 D • ₹ 295/- (HB)

4138 B Rs. 250 (PB)

4181 C • ₹ 195/-

4177 B • ₹ 195/-

9997 C • ₹ 80/-

4182 D • ₹ 96/-

9984 E • ₹ 399/- (HB)

4130 B • ₹ 120/-

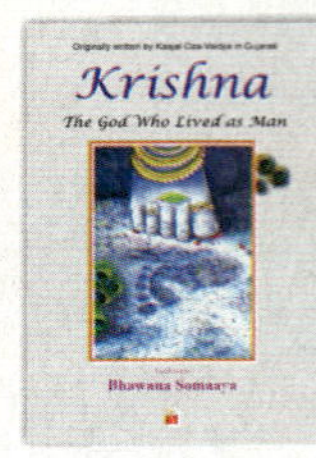

4183 A • ₹ 350/- (HB)

4151 A • ₹ 399/- (HB)

9811 P • ₹ 120/-

9585 A • ₹ 96/-

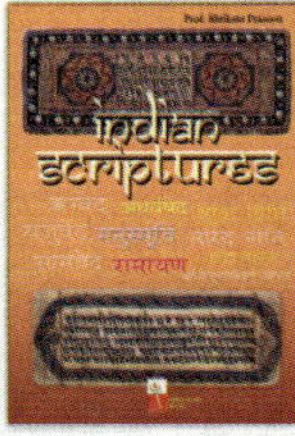

9405 A • ₹ 195/-

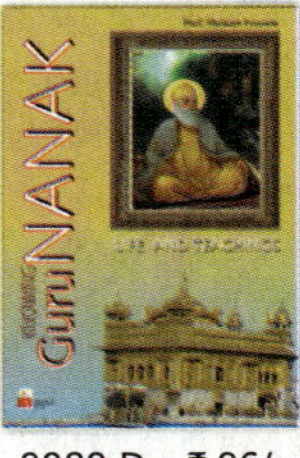

9989 D • ₹ 96/-

9508 D • ₹ 95/-

4134 B • ₹ 80/-

4188 A • ₹ 160/-

9504 D • ₹ 100/-

4133 A • ₹ 60/-

9513 A • ₹ 195/-

4126 B • ₹ 96/-

9812 R • ₹ 120/-

4152 B • ₹ 96/-

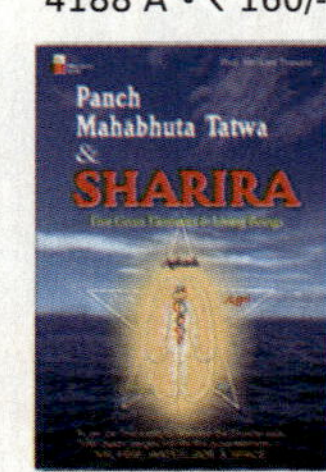

4407 C • ₹ 195/-

9504 D • ₹ 100/-

4124 A • ₹ 120/-

9513 A • ₹ 175/-

9520 D • ₹ 120/-

9987 E • ₹ 150/-

8898 D • ₹ 80/-

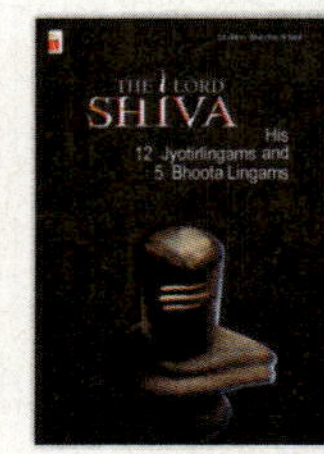

4190 C • ₹ 160/-

9509 A • ₹ 150/-

9510 B • ₹ 120/-

9525 A • ₹ 150/-

9540 D • ₹ 150/-

9542 B • ₹ 150/-

9514 B • ₹ 60/-

4132 D • ₹ 100/-

9069 A • ₹ 80/-

ASTROLOGY/VASTU/HYPNOTISM/PAMISTRY

9871 A • ₹ 240/-

9693 H • ₹ 195/-

9671 F • ₹ 195/-

2127 D • ₹ 150/-

4177 C • ₹ 195/-

9086 A • ₹ 295/-HB

2116 D • ₹ 150/-

8259 D • ₹ 88/-

2109 F • ₹ 150/-

2112 D • ₹ 120/-

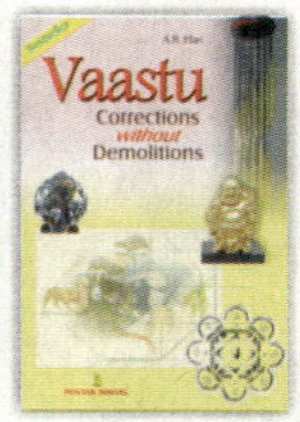

3110 B • ₹ 100/-

2133 B • ₹ 96/-

8899 D • ₹ 110/-

2125 D • ₹ 80/-

8925 D • ₹ 96/-

2132 A • ₹ 150/-

9432 D • ₹ 150/-

2120 D • ₹ 150/-

2109 F • ₹ 100/-

ENGLISH IMPROVEMENT

7540 D • ₹ 175/-

5541 C • ₹ 196/-

6651 E • ₹ 175/-

9448 D • ₹ 175/-

9056 A • ₹ 125/-

5538 D • ₹ 100/-

PERSON & PERSONALITIES

9669 D • ₹ 120/-

9825 E • ₹ 150/-

2113 D • ₹ 195/-

9764 R • ₹ 100/-

8991 D • ₹ 120/-

BODY/BEAUTY CARE

3093 D • ₹ 150/-

9986 B • ₹ 150/-

8971 B • ₹ 120/-

9922 F • ₹ 120/-

8865 F • ₹ 120/-

JOKES HUMOUR & SATIRE

2342 C • ₹ 100/-
2343 D • ₹ 100/-
2341 B • ₹ 60/-
2318 A • ₹ 96/-
2330 B • ₹ 96/-
2319 B • ₹ 96/-

FICTION

Set Code SH 001

THREE BOOKS — William Shakespeare — Set Price ₹ 297/- ₹ 99/- Each Volume
Set Code 9795 A

THREE BOOKS — Munshi PREMCHAND
Set Code 9752 B • ₹ 550/-

PARENTING

9906 J • ₹ 175/- (HB)

8261 D • ₹ 180/-

9674 J • ₹ 220/-

9784 J • ₹ 150/-

LISTEN TO ME, MY DEAR YOUNG CHILD
9594 K • ₹ 80/-

The Art of Successful Parenting
8917 D • ₹ 120/-

FUN, FACTS, MAGIC & MYSTERIES

9484 B • ₹ 150/-

2275 D • ₹ 120/-

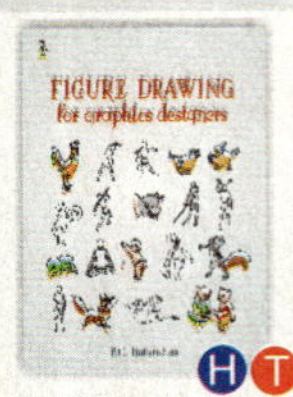

9479 M • ₹. 120/-

9470 B • ₹ 100/-

2208 M • ₹ 100/-

9816 D • ₹ 100/-

2247 F • ₹ 100/-

2250 A • ₹ 110/-

2211 F • ₹ 100/-

9457 E • ₹ 150/-

2237 M • ₹ 80/-

2335 A • ₹ 80/-

2243 L • ₹ 100/-

9775 M • ₹ 100/-

9985 A • ₹ 80/-

5110 A • ₹ 80/-

2337 C • ₹ 96/-

2336 B • ₹ 100/-

2331 C • ₹ 100/-

9977 B • ₹ 100/-

YOGA & MEDITATION

8269 A • ₹ 195/-

9998 D • ₹ 120/-

8939 D • ₹ 96/-

9080 C • ₹ 24/-

9958 S • ₹ 160/-

9087 B • ₹ 120/-

2118 F • ₹ 120/-

8901 D • ₹ 150/-

8099 D • ₹ 80/-

9025 D • ₹ 80/-

HOMEOPATHY, AYURDEDA

9446 B • ₹ 150/-

8887 D • ₹ 175/-

8270 B • ₹ 165/-

8923 D • ₹ 195/-

8010 D • ₹ 96/-

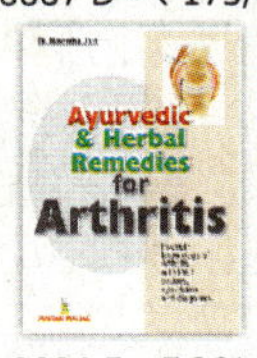

9094 E • ₹ 96/-

8944 D • ₹ 175/-

8948 A • ₹ 120/-

WORLD FAMOUS SERIES

9472 D • ₹ 100/-

2337 C • ₹ 100/-

9483 A • Rs. 100/-

51107 • ₹ 100/-

9766 A • Rs. 100/-

9489 G • Rs. 100/-

9761 M • Rs. 100/-

World Famous Mysterious Objects
True Stories of Mowglis and other Wild Childrens
World Famous Treasures (Lost and Found)
World Famous WARs & Battles
True Stories of Mystic Places
World Famous Adventures
World Famous Military Operations
World Famous Spy Scandals
World Famous Spies & Spymasters
World Famous Crooks & Con Men
True Stories 81 Weird Humans
True Stories of Great Explorers
World Famous Ghosts
World Famous Strange Mysteries
and many more.......

₹ 100/- each book

LOVE, ROMANCE & SEX

9602 B • Rs. 125/-

8260 D • Rs. 96/-

8266 D • Rs. 80/-

8278 C • Rs. 100/-

8916 D • Rs. 120/-

MORAL, WISDOM & FAIRY TALES

9677 P • Rs. 150/-

9486 D • Rs. 250/-

9763 P • Rs. 150/-

8967 F • Rs. 80/-

9077 E • Rs.120/-

9563 N • Rs. 12